# TRAINS OF CUBA

## *Steam, Diesel & Electric*

**Adolf Hungry Wolf**

Canadian Caboose Press

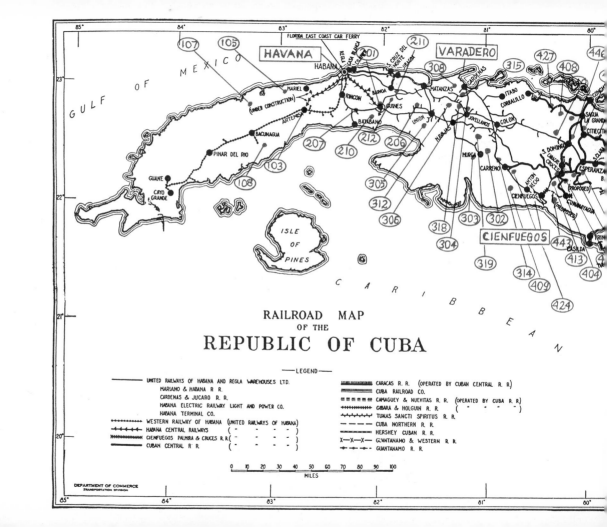

# RAILROAD MAP
## OF THE
# REPUBLIC OF CUBA

—LEGEND—

| | |
|---|---|
| ———— UNITED RAILWAYS OF HABANA AND REGLA WAREHOUSES LTD. | CARACAS R. R. (OPERATED BY CUBAN CENTRAL R. R.) |
| MARIANO & HABANA R. R. | CUBA RAILROAD CO. |
| CARDENAS & JUCARO R. R. | CAMAGUEY & NUEVITAS R. R. (OPERATED BY CUBA R. R.) |
| HABANA ELECTRIC RAILWAY LIGHT AND POWER CO. | GIBARA & HOLGUIN R. R. ( " - " ) |
| HABANA TERMINAL CO. | TUNAS SANCTI SPIRITUS R. R. |
| +++++ WESTERN RAILWAY OF HABANA (UNITED RAILWAYS OF HABANA) | CUBA NORTHERN R. R. |
| ++++ HABANA CENTRAL RAILWAYS ( " - " ) | HERSHEY CUBAN R. R. |
| ++++ CIENFUEGOS PALMIRA & CRUCES R. R. ( " - " ) | X—X—X GUANTANAMO & WESTERN R. R. |
| ———— CUBAN CENTRAL R. R. | GUANTANAMO R. R. |

0  10  20  30  40  50  60  70  80  90  100
MILES

DEPARTMENT OF COMMERCE
TRANSPORTATION DIVISION

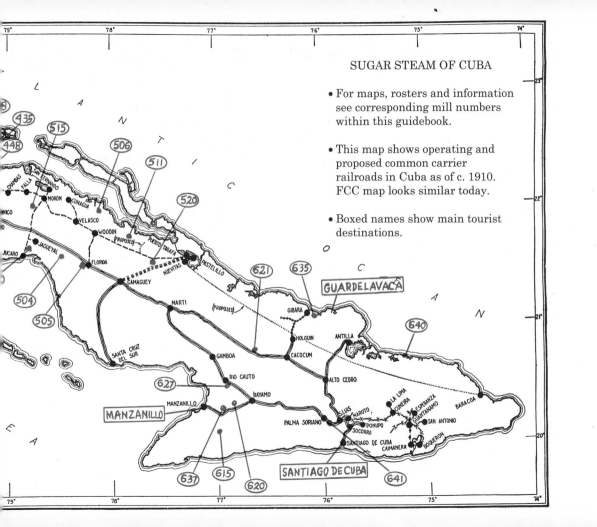

SUGAR STEAM OF CUBA

- For maps, rosters and information
  see corresponding mill numbers
  within this guidebook.

- This map shows operating and
  proposed common carrier
  railroads in Cuba as of c. 1910.
  FCC map looks similar today.

- Boxed names show main tourist
  destinations.

To receive our
**free newsletter**
about current events in
Cuban railroading,
send a stamped,
self-addressed envelope to:

**Canadian Caboose Press
Box 844
Skookumchuck, B.C.
V0B 2E0, Canada.**

*We'll tell you about*

★ Sugar mill operations, motive power changes and

★ SPECIAL TOUR PROGRAMS
*We'll also include*

★ Our latest book and video list, plus

★ A discount offer for our various
Cuban railroading video programs, and

★ Information about our full colour book:
CUBAN HOLIDAY,
*Travelling Through a Transportation Timewarp*
by Adolf Hungry Wolf

*Front Cover: Two of Central Mal Tiempo's narrow gauge Baldwin Consolidations face off on the mainline at the edge of town, while on the road are a couple of horse drawn carriages, a cowboy, and a blue and white '51 Chevy. This is typical Cuban transportation in the 1990's.*
*Inset scenes: The afternoon train from Nuevitas to Moron makes a last station stop at Patria before pulling up to the large, classic depot in Moron. General Electric No. 50909 was built in 1955. Budd RDC's are being used as coaches behind the lightweight baggage car. The other scene shows Hershey Electric Brill interurban car No. 3010, waiting to depart from the branchline terminus at Santa Cruz del Norte.*
*Back cover: Cuba's two largest steam locomotives - and its only 2-8-2 types - doublehead upgrade to Central Ifrain Alfonso.*
All four, AHW Photos

**Printed and bound in Canada**

Copyright © 1996 by Adolf Hungry Wolf.
All rights reserved.
This book may not be reproduced in any way.
First Printing 1996
Canadian Cataloguing in Publication Data
Hungry Wolf, Adolf, 1944-
Trains of Cuba
Includes Index
**ISBN 0-920698-46-8**
1. Railroads--Cuba--Guidebooks.
2. Cuba--Guidebooks, I.  Title.
HE2868.H86 1996 385'.097291  C96-910643-2

# Preface and Acknowledgments

This is the book I wish I could have had for my first visit to Cuba a few years ago. Instead, I had to rely on a variety of photocopied maps and handwritten information that came from friends who had already been there. Unfortunately, the main one of these must remain nameless since his government doesn't know that when he flies down to Mexico City on vacation each year he goes on to spend a few weeks in Cuba, where he's among the most enthused of many visiting railfans from all over the world. My sons and I hereby give you our heartfelt thanks, friend, and no doubt we speak for many others whom you've helped as well. I hope this book passes your knowledgeable inspection! (As an aside, in Cuba they don't insist on stamping passports.)

For historical information I'm especially indebted to Wayne Weiss of Bellaire Roundhouse, David Thornhill of *World Steam*, and Jim Hutzler of Rail Study Tours. All three have made important contributions to the assembling of a complete Cuban Steam Roster. The most thorough version so far published is *Industrial Steam Locomotives of Cuba*, compiled by G.A.P. Leach and produced by the Industrial Railway Society of London. A major source of map information for many years has been the renowned news magazine *World Steam*. Many detailed maps have has also been published within Cuba and can still be found in bookstalls there.

Most photos in this volume were taken during several trips to Cuba that I made with my sons Okan and Iniskim. We all traded cameras, lenses and films, making many of the resulting pictures a joint effort. Initials will tell you which one of us took specific scenes, in those cases where we know for sure. We also shot over 40 hours of video tape, much of which was Okan's work.

This book is being produced in cooperation with Minaz, Cuba's Ministry of Sugar, through the efforts of Elio Leal Groverau, Chief of Protocol, and Vincente Barreneche, Chief of International Relations.

Similar assistance was provided by the offices of FCC director Sr. Ing. Pastar Fleites, especially Osvaldo Herrera.

A special dedication to the many wonderful friends my boys and I have met aboard the trains of Cuba, and along the tracks. We want to especially thank the following, in no particular order: Efren Figueredo, Fabio Correa Sosa, Armando Barnada Carvajal, Luis Pascual and Luisa Debasa, Rodolfo Betancourt, mi familia en La caridad de Bariay, Yoel Peres Ramires and Luis Blanco.

These pages will also introduce the work of Cuban photo-reporter Israel Wilfredo Diaz Gomez, better know as "Wildy," Cuba's first notable rail-fan, inspired and encouraged by many visiting friends and fans.

Thanks also to: my wife Beverly, along with sons Okan and Iniskim, for going with me on some of these trips, and for helping with parts of the work; Dianne Jefferson of Communications Plus for book design and production; Brian Clarkson of Cranbrook Foto for colour prints; Lou Mellencamp for black and white prints; and Baker Street Uniglobe for flight arrangements.

*A meeting at the Junction of Cuba's most photogenic railway. Santa Lucia No. 4, a handsome, cap-stacked 2 1/2-foot gauge Baldwin 2-8-0 built in 1919 and originally named "Guabajaney," waits in the siding at Bariay - with distinctive "La Teta" rising from a green forested base to a rocky point in the background - while a cane train arrives from the far end of the mainline behind one of Central Rafael Freyre's 7 narrow gauge Consolidations.*   A&OHW photo

# Introduction

Cuba is the last place on earth where you can go and watch several different 100 year old American made steam locomotives performing their daily work just as they've always done. Nearby are ox-teams, horse drawn carriages and a wide assortment of old American cars and trucks. It is truly amazing that only 90 miles from the coast of Florida is a land that still has several hundred steam engines hauling trains, often on picturesque routes that have hardly been seen or photographed by outsiders.

In addition to the steam there's an old electric railroad built by the Hershey Chocolate Company to haul sugar and other products to the ships at port and to provide freight and passenger service for neighbors and employees, service that continues with some of the original General Electric steeplecab locomotives and Brill interurban cars.

The electric lines and most of the steam powered sugar railroads are interconnected via the country's far flung national railroad system called the FCC, or Ferrocarriles de Cuba. Although more modern and international in equipment than other rail attractions, Cuba's dieselized national line nevertheless offers a wide variety of freight and passenger trains hauled by motive power that includes American GE diesels from the 50's and Alco-style MLW's sent down by Canada in the 70's. Photogenic train stations abound, some of them real architectural gems, as do semaphores and elevated control towers, all of which help to make train photography a growing interest for visitors to Cuba.

# Photographing Trains in Cuba

A major concern for first time visitors is whether they will be allowed to use their cameras while travelling around Cuba, and the answer is a resounding yes! Official policy says you may take pictures of anything except military subjects and certain places of national security. Unfortunately, the latter category does include railroads and sugar mills to some degree, so if you have a particular desire to photograph these, it would be advisable to learn beforehand about local regulations, else to join a tour group, which will probably have the necessary authorizations. Snap photos to your heart's content of trains running out in the country, or at railroad stations, especially the steam powered trains in the cane fields. Tourism is an important source of income for Cuba and it has been officially recognized that photographing trains is a popular goal for many tourists.

There was a period of some 20 years in recent Cuban history when hardly any photos were taken of Cuban trains, especially on the more isolated sugar lines; little knowledge of their operations filtered out during that time into the rail enthusiast world. Thus it has surprised many to learn about the large variety of old American locomotives still at work in Cuba, especially when they hear that they can now go and visit those same locomotives and photograph them, perhaps even arrange to ride behind one of them. Cuban ministry officials have expressed interest in meeting legitimate tourist requests.

That sugar is still Cuba's number one crop helps to keep its mills and railroads on security alert. There have been numerous attempts at sabotage over the years; as recently as 1994 one man was arrested for throwing an iron rod into the main gears of a sugar mill, thus putting that mill and its surrounding community out of commission for the rest of the harvest. If you find that security concerns get in the way of your photo desires, try to be understanding of those who are in charge. With nearly everything changing in Cuba, expect that photographing old trains will continue to get easier and better.

Cubans are the most photo friendly people you could hope to encounter, unlike the people of many countries where a camera gets dirty looks and hidden faces. Consider giving some kind of present after taking someone's picture, something useful like a pen or lighter, else a bit of money if nothing else is at hand. When given as a gesture of friendship, rather than as any sort of bribe, the gift is highly appreciated, since life there offers very little in money or materials. I recommend the same gift treatment for anyone who helps you in any sort of way. It takes so little to repay the many kindnesses you will be shown.

As a foreigner you must be prepared for a great deal of attention coming from a people yearning to learn more about your part of the world. If you park your car while waiting to take a train photo, there's a good chance it will soon be surrounded by curious and friendly faces. Some will want to know if you need help, others may wish to practice their English, while most simply want to watch and see what a tourist looks and acts like, up close. I have witnessed foreigners hurridly roll up their windows or otherwise work hard at ignoring these crowds, but I can tell you from personal experience that the best response is to say a big cheerful hello, tell them what country you're from, explain that you are about to take some photos of their local train and then go do your work. If the train is long in coming - and those people can probably tell you so - you develop some track-side friendships that may well turn out to be even more valuable than the pictures.

I would be remiss not to warn you about "Chicle!" It's an expression you'll hear over and over, at track-side and most everywhere else. It's mostly called out by kids who'd like you to give them some gum, or any other treat you might have with you. It's impossible to carry enough for them all; many tourists just say no, period. I always carry candies (available by the sackful at most hotel stores), but give them only to kids who are nice, especially ones who behave while I'm trying to take some important picture. Explain what you want them to do or not to do before the train arrives, then reward them afterwards if you want. Pens and paper are more practical alternatives to sweets, and just as much appreciated. Don't scorn Cuba's kids just because they crowd around you the moment you arrive. Consider their attention to be a form of honor and most likely that's what it will turn out to be. Some guys no doubt worry their ulcers over this constant, unrequested attention, so be forewarned. Keep in mind that a polite "no," accompanied by a smile, is accepted by most kids, though sometimes it's admittedly a challenge to be that nice at the end of a long, hot day during which you've had two flat tires and missed several fine photo scenes. This is all part of what makes the trains of Cuba so adventurous.

*Cameras are rare in the hands of Cubans and film even more so, resulting in many requests from people wishing to have their picture taken. Return visits are enhanced by generous gifts of the resulting prints. Railroad crews thus remembered may repay the kindness with some special treat or other that will long be remembered. This scene was taken during a ride down a narrow gauge branchline.*
AHW Photo

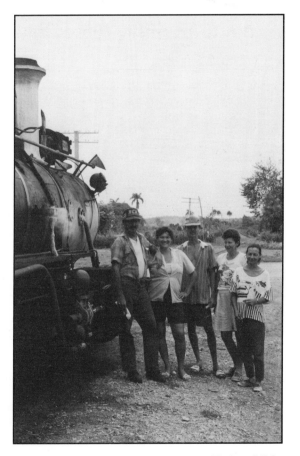

*Trains of Cuba*

# Planning Your Trip

If you live anywhere other than the U.S. there's no problem flying to Cuba, where several airports are set up to receive international flights. If you're married and want to bring along the family, it's possible to spend a nice week on the Caribbean and still get your fill of steam railroading. Most of the main tourist resorts and hotels are within a short drive of active steam. Fares for the flight and basic costs for hotels and meals are about average for a Caribbean destination nowadays. There are some very cheap hotels in the country, but these cater mainly to Cuban vacationers and offer facilities and services probably lower than most tourists will accept. However, such hotels can be handy for the more hardy who wish to spend several days at some particular remote sugar operation without driving back and forth to a resort.

And driving is the main way for train seekers to get around, particularly those wanting to visit the better sugar steam operations. Although FCC trains can be used to reach many sugar mills, it is not always possible to photograph active steam there, so a car must be used to get out on the line. If money is of no concern, you can always rent a taxi in any populated area, but this will cost far more than rental cars. There are now several car agencies in Cuba, with most hotels having a desk for at least one of them. Daily rates at this time are about $60 U.S. and up, with the recent change to unlimited mileage being of great help. Another option is to negotiate a fare with the driver of most any private car. Do keep in mind that what you pay for one day of a rental car represents more U.S. cash than most Cubans have any hope of obtaining....and they all know that. Though crime is still rare, especially compared

to other Latin countries, the natural human look of longing isn't. You'll be seeing it a lot.

Roads in Cuba are generally not bad, with motor vehicle traffic minimal, but you'll be sharing space with all sorts of other transportation including very slow moving ox teams (totally unlit at night!), slightly faster horses with wagons and carriages, numerous barely-running old automobiles, and endless hordes of bicyclers who will absolutely refuse to move over and give up the right of way. Night driving is not recommended; there are few lights along the roadways, and none on many of the conveyances. Fuel, food and refreshments are generally available only in the larger towns and near tourist resorts, rarely in the vicinity of sugar mills, though in a bind you can try to shop for these among the locals.

Booking a vacation package well ahead of time can save a lot of money, especially if any part of your family comes along. It does however limit your mobility in case the weather turns unfavorable or the steam you made plans for turns out not to be working. The sugar harvest generally runs from about the first of the year until April or May, though this depends a lot on the rains, which are variable, and on other conditions. This is the "mild" season for Cuba, but that still means hot for visitors. Roads for seeing steam at work are usually remote and dusty; always carry water, spare clothing and emergency supplies. With enough rain these roads become impassable, in which case you hunker down at your hotel with a good book, else move to a different part of the island. Be sure to bring all the film and photo items you'll need, as they are scarce in Cuba. Also bring prints of trains you've photographed elsewhere to give to new friends.

Ask for a highway map when you rent your car, then combine it with the maps and directions in this book, which should get you to most of what you find listed herein. While some marathon photographers take pride in photographing 100 or more working steam locomotives on a single three or four week trip, others prefer to visit just a few mills so they can spend more time at each, becoming friends with the people and bringing home far more than just a big pile of steam engine pictures.

*One of the most popular destinations for early rail photographers who came to Cuba in the 1980's was Central Esteban Hernandez, whose 30" gauge line near Santa Clara not only boasted a varied fleet of interesting steam engines (including three tiny Vulcan 0-4-0 tankers), but also the only tunnel on a sugar railroad. Regrettably, by the time of this 1993 photo the steam was lined up and rusting on the backtrack, while Russian diesels like the one on the very left had taken over. Still in service, and almost as historic as the steam, are a pair of Brookville switchers painted silver and carrying their original nameplates. "Nuarbe," on the right, came here new to Central Guipuzcoa in 1935 while "Alameda" followed in 1937. The line's favorite engine is a 6-wheeled diesel built by the Canadian Locomotive Company in 1958.*
IHW photo

*Trains of Cuba*

# Ferrocarriles de Cuba

There is a general perception that the Caribbean islands have no railways, or at best some little obscure sugar lines. One glance at the current timetable book of the FCC - Ferrocarriles de Cuba - will alter that image forever. The volume is No. 12, issued September 24, 1995, and it consists of 226 jam-packed pages listing the schedules and operations of numerous passenger, freight and mixed trains. I've spent hours studying that volume of late, trying to figure out which information might be of interest or value to those of you reading this guidebook. Public timetables are often difficult to come by once you're in Cuba, so I'll pass on some sample schedules for various trips, keeping in mind that these are all subject to change.

The various railroads that have been amalgamated into today's Ferrocarriles de Cuba were nearly dieselized by the time of the 1959 Revolution, with the last FCC steam work done by some dock switchers in Havana around 1970. However, many sugar mills run their steam powered trains over FCC tracks to reach cane fields and reload points, thus steam can still be seen passing FCC stations and at times even performing FCC freight work.

An eclectic assortment of international diesels are keeping today's FCC trains on the move, including vintage General Motors units from the 1950's and the Canadian MLW-built Alco types from the 70's, along with machines from France, Hungary, Czechoslovakia and the USSR. Colour photographers delight in the many colour schemes, which are not only tasteful and photogenic but also identify the various locomotive classes.

One set of Alco FA's remained in passenger service out of San Luis into the 1980s, but these have since been withdrawn, along with most other Alcos (and all Baldwins) for lack of parts. There is an effort underway to repair at least one of these FA's for possible charter train service. There are also Brill rail-buses from the 1930's that may be rebuilt for charter work, as several still operate on remote branch lines mainly around Guantanamo. Unfortunately, none of the classic Mack rail-buses have so far been located, though these served on light branch lines into the 1960's.

The FCC has actually considered a return to some steam power in recent years, due to limited funds for diesel upkeep and replacement. First there was talk of trading sugar to East Germany for a fleet of World War II 2-10-0's just being taken out of service, though they burned coal, a fuel Cuba finds hard to get. Then there were discussions with China of a similar trade for new steam locomotives which that country still builds. For now, the FCC has followed a less costly and more low key program towards potential steam power, though it is a program that would surely make world news if it indeed developed. For the past few years the FCC has hired, on contract, Argentina's famed L. Dante Porta, considered the world's leading expert on modern steam technology, who has led a small Cuban work force in the total rebuilding and modernizing of a 1919 Alco 2-8-0 at the FCC's Sagua La Grande workshops, which are known for helping sugar mills rebuild their steam engines. No. 1816 worked for Central Unidad Proletario before being drafted by the FCC for this experimental rebuilding. *If* the locomotive is successful - that is, fuel efficient, reliable and strong enough for regular yard and branch line work - then plans call for a

selection of 100 standard gauge sugar mill locomotives (mainly of 2-6-0 and 2-8-0 wheel arrangements) to receive similar rebuildings, after which they would work for their mills during
the four to five month sugar harvest, then haul
trains on the FCC for the rest of the year. It is
hard to calculate what world wide interest might
be aroused by the idea of 100 freight and passenger trains hauled by 70 and 80 year old
American steam locomotives!

The FCC actually does have one steam locomotive already in operation, a 1919 Baldwin
Mogul all spiffed up to haul tourists on a short,
scenic stretch of track out of the historic colo-
nial town of Trinidad, near the Escambray
Mountains. 2-6-0 No. 1551 was built as Cuban
American Sugar Company No. 8, but worked
much of its life for Central Ramon Ponciano in
the province of Sancti Spiritus. This is expected to be only the first of several potential
steam-powered tourist runs in Cuba, with some vintage American
passenger cars available.

Cuba's rolling stock, like the motive power, has an international flavor, with coaches coming from builders in Spain, Italy,
Germany, Argentina and Cuba, plus some heavyweight survivors
from the U.S. Freight cars are mostly of European style and make,
though again some old American cars remain, along with a busy
fleet of Cuban-made cabooses.

Trains may be photographed in most locations, though current

*Devotees of Alco power will
be pleased to know that Cuban railroaders consider the
MX624 model built by Mon-
treal Locomotive Works to be
the No. 1 locomotive in Cuba.
Canada's sale of 50 such engines to the island in 1975
created an uproar in some
American political circles.
The throb of their 2600 hp
engines can be heard in all
major terminals, among their
regular assignments being the
overnight express trains between Havana and Santiago
de Cuba. This scene shows
the rear car of such an express, ready to leave from
downtown Havana's Estacion
Central, while beside it stands
MLW No. 52431.*
A&OHW Photo

schedules are not easy to come by, making it difficult to plan line-
side pictures. In many places the tracks allow faster speeds than
nearby roads, so train chasing can also be difficult. Some of the
stations are very handsome and well maintained, often with horse
drawn carriages and old American cars parked as taxis outside.
Some cities have roundhouses with turntables, but access to them
is quite restricted, as are visits to the main FCC shops in Havana
and Camaguey. The best opportunities are provided for guided tour
groups, and these visits are on the increase.

The country's overnight express between Havana and Santiago de Cuba - Train Nos. 1 and 2 - provides a memorable experience, though for many people it is more of an endurance ride than a recommended way to see Cuba. Having neither sleepers nor dining cars makes the train's scheduled 14 hours quite long (16 hours, the last time I rode it in 1996), though the seats have lots of leg room, are soft and reclining. Two fellows with a cart offer small sandwiches, oranges and potent Cuban coffee, while local entrepreneurs are now allowed to sell their homemade eats to passengers during station stops. Food and bottled water is best brought along, as are warm clothing or a blanket, since the air conditioned cars tend to become quite cold at night.

A better choice for tourists wanting to see the heart of Cuba by train is the weekly special service offered by FCC aboard a rebuilt Fiat rail-bus, with a capacity of 38 passengers, reclining seats, wide vision windows, snack bar and music, plus a relatively rapid daytime schedule of only 9 or 10 hours. This machine is available for charter trips anywhere on the FCC system and can be used by tour groups to visit some steam powered sugar lines. Our newsletter will update you on this.

FCC branch lines often have passenger service as well, though this is mainly to bring workers to and from their homes, towns and factories, so that times, destinations and connections are not usually favorable to tourists. Trains on busy branch lines tend to be made up of demotored Budd RDC's or strings of converted boxcars, often hauled by American made General Motors G-8 type locomotives in a tasteful green and yellow paint scheme. Less busy lines are served by a big fleet of simple rail-buses made in Cuba from Hungarian plans and parts.

The accompanying schedules and rosters are far from complete, but will serve to give you an idea of railroading on the FCC.

*The passenger yard at Santiago de Cuba always has an international mix of baggage cars and coaches, as seen here in this 1995 view that includes two old American heavyweights, on the right, plus cars built in Argentina and Cuba.*
A& OHW Photo

*Trains of Cuba*

*Trackside at the FCC station in Santiago de Cuba. Russian built TEM-15K No. 81001, painted chocolate brown with yellow stripes, waits for work along with an old American heavyweight baggage car, painted green with a silver roof. The passenger station on the left faces a wide and busy street, while the freight warehouse at right sits alongside the harbor docks in Santiago Bay.*
AHW Photo

# FCC LOCOMOTIVE FLEET

| Type | Builder | Country | Date | HP | Weight | Road Nos. | Type of Service |
|------|---------|---------|------|-----|--------|-----------|-----------------|
| GM-900 | General Motors | USA | 1955 | 820 | 72t | 50901-50941 | Medium |
| MX624 | Montreal Locomotive Works | Canada | 1975 | 2600 | 112t | 52401-52450 | Heavy |
| M60 | Brissoneau et Lotz | France | 1965 | 830 | 72t | 50801-50830 | Medium |
| Electric | General Electric | USA | 1920 to 1926 | 820 | 55t | 20801-20808 21001-21004 21201-21203 | Light |
| TEM-4 | Brynansk | USSR | 1964 | 1000 | 120t | 51001-51040 | Heavy |
| T-458 | Ceskomoravska-Kolben Damek, Prague | Chekoslovakia | 1964 | 660 | 74 t | 50701-50720 | Medium |
| DVM-9 | Ganz-Mavag | Hungary | 1969 | 830 | 76t | 61001-61070 | Medium |
| TGM-25 | | USSR | 1970 | 400 | 46t | 30401-30438 | Light |
| M62-K | Kolomna | USSR | 1974 | 1680 | 120t | 61601-61620 | Heavy |
| TEM-2TK | Brynansk | USSR | 1974 | 1030 | 120t | 71001-71079 | Heavy |
| TGM-8K | | USSR | 1977 | 800 | 80t | 38000 Series (Minaz) | Heavy |
| TGM-4 | | USSR | 1978 | 750 | 68t | 37000 Series (Minaz) | Medium |
| TE-114K | Voroshilovgrad | USSR | 1978 | 2500 | 120t | 52601-52699 | Heavy |
| TEM-15K | | USSR | 1988 | 1030 | 108t | 81001-81025 | Medium |
| TGM-6 | | USSR | 1990 | 1200 | 90t | 39000 Series (Minaz) | Heavy |

| FCC RAIL-BUS FLEET | | | | | | |
|---|---|---|---|---|---|---|
| Model | Builder | Country | Date | HP | Wt. | Speed |
| Model 55 | Brill | USA | 1930 | 120/240 | 52 | 50 |
| RDC | Budd | USA | 1952 | 550 | 55 | 105 |
| Electric | Brill | USA | 1917 | 250 | 46 | 50 |
| Pionero | FCC | Cuba | 1970 | 120 | 20 | 50 |
| Guerrillero | FCC | Cuba | 1970 | 240 | 35 | 50 |
| Motor coach | Fiat | Argentina | 1976 | 500 | 57.3 | 115 |
| Ligero | Taino | Cuba | 1987 | 240 | | |
| DR-6 | | USSR | 1990 | 1000 | 58 | 120 |
| DR-6 Trailer | | USSR | 1990 | | 36.5 | |

*Hecho en Cuba - Railbus No. 4120 is part of a large fleet built in FCC shops using basic parts made in Hungary, serving lightly travelled branch lines all over the country. The blue and white machine was stopped at the quaint Progreso station, which is also passed frequently by the well-kept steam locomotives of Central Jose Smith Comas, located a short distance away.*
IHW Photo

*Trains of Cuba*

# FCC PASSENGER EQUIPMENT

| Builder | Model | Country | Weight | Max. allowed speed |
|---|---|---|---|---|
| Fiat | Air conditioned | Argentina | 42 | 100 |
| Fiat | Ventinilla | Argentina | 39 | 100 |
| Fiat | Furgon | Argentina | 39 | 100 |
| Fiat | Comedor | Argentina | 42 | 100 |
| Taino | Express Coach | Cuba | 40 | 80 |
| Fiat | Coach | Italy | 40 | 65 |
| Various | Steel heavyweight coaches | USA | 75 | 50 |
| Budd | light coaches | USA | 52 | 70 |
| Uerdin-Gen. | coaches | Germany | 50 | 50 |
| | coaches | Romania | 24 | 50 |
| | coaches | Spain | 40 | 70 |
| Various | Heavyweight Baggage cars | USA | 60 | 50 |
| Various | "Commando coaches" | USA | 30 | 50 |
| Various | Rebuilt from old boxcars | USA | 30 | 50 |
| Taino | "Pionero" | Cuba | 30 | 50 |
| Taino | "Pionero-light" | Cuba | 20 | 50 |
| Brill | | USA | 50 | 50 |

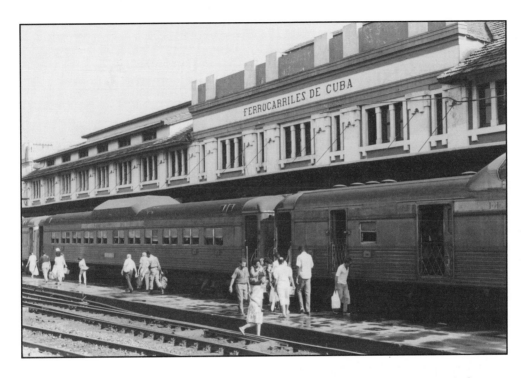

*Many Cuban railway stations are architectural landmarks, such as this imposing two-story structure in downtown Camaguey. Passengers are leaving a branch-line passenger train that has just reached its destination from Nuevitas with a typical consist of seven demotored Budd RDC's hauled by a single green and yellow General Electric G8 export engine. The whole scene was like vintage American railroading of the 1950's, with a distinct Caribbean flavor. No other country still provides such an experience.* A&OHW Photo

**19** *Trains of Cuba*

| Cross-country Fiat Rail-bus Service | | | | | |
|---|---|---|---|---|---|
| *Eastbound* | | | | | *Westbound* |
| Read Down | $ US | Station | Kms. | $US | Read up |
| 10:30 | 0.00 | Havana | 0.0 | 35.00 | 21.08 |
| 12:00 | 12.00 | Santa Clara | 281 | 24.00 | 19.41 |
| 16:23 | 22.00 | Camaguey | 537 | 13.00 | 1714 |
| 21:17 | 35.00 | Santiago de Cuba | 854 | 0.0 | 13.28 |
| | | **Runs weekly** | | | |

| Cuba's Overnight Express-Train Nos. 1 & 2 | | | | |
|---|---|---|---|---|
| Read down | $ US | Station | $US | Read up |
| 16:25 | 0.00 | Havana | 35.00 | 07:05 |
| 18:00 | 6:00 | Matanzas | 31.00 | 05:27 |
| 20:33 | 12:00 | Santa Clara | 24.00 | 02:53 |
| 23:13 | 18:00 | Ciego de Avila | 17.00 | 00:13 |
| 01:14 | 22:00 | Camaguey | 13.00 | 22:23 |
| 03:01 | 27.00 | Las Tunas | 9.00 | 20:19 |
| 06:45 | 35.00 | Santiago de Cuba | | 16:35 |

Passenger Train No. 414 departs Santiago de Cuba at 13:35, arrives San Luis 14:24, and terminates at Guantanamo at 17:29.
Train 403 Leaves Guantanamo at 04:55, arrives in San Luis at 07:43 and terminates at Santiago de Cuba at 09:00.
A total of 39 trains are scheduled in and out of Guantanamo on short-haul railbus service.

*Two FCC express trains are seen at the important station stop of San Luis, where tracks head out in several directions. The dark green cars with beige stripes are air conditioned 42-ton units built by Fiat in Argentina.*
AHW Photo

*Trains of Cuba*

## Holguin Connection

| Read Down | | | | Read Up | |
|---|---|---|---|---|---|
| Frt. 1301 | Psgr. 431 | Station | Km. | Psgr. 430 | Frt. 1302 |
| 00:20 | 13:10 | Las Tunas | 370.7 | 11:57 | 02:01 |
| 01:05 | 13:53 | Omaja | 401.6 | 11.14 | 01:04 |
| 02:21 | 15:11 | Cacocun | 448.1 | 09:53 | 23:58 |
| | 16:00 | Holguin | 17.8 | 09:05 | |

This service connects the mainline express at Las Tunas with Holguin, near the favorite rail destination of Rafael Freyre. Several trains run daily, along with others connecting Holguin to Santiago de Cuba. There used to be 3-foot gauge freight and passenger service offered from Holguin north to the Atlantic port at Gibara, connecting with the Rafael Freyre line along the way, but this ended around 1970. Note that Cacocun is a junction on the northern FCC mainline where the branch connects to Holguin.

---

Passenger Train No. 408 leaves Santiago de Cuba at 06:05 and arrives Manzanillo at 12:10. No. 409 departs Manzanillo at 14:10 and arrives at Santiago de Cuba at 20:15.
Train No. 410 leaves Santiago de Cuba at 08:20 and arrives Holguin at 11:35. No. 411 leaves Holguin at 14:35 and arrives at Santiago de Cuba at 17:55.

## Branchline Round Trip

| Train 130 | Station | Km. | Train 129 |
|---|---|---|---|
| 08:50 | Guareiras | 8.7 | 08:24 |
| 09:10 | Colon | 0.0 | 08:05 |
| 09:30 | Altamisal | 13.1 | 07:37 |
| 10:05 | Maximo Gomez | 25.4 | 07:10 |
| 10:54 | Cardenas | 48.8 | 06:20 |
| | | | Train starts here |

This is an interesting round trip that can be done in an easy morning from the tourist beach resort of Varadero. Take a taxi for the 15 minute drive to Cardenas and board at one of Cuba's oldest train stations, then end up at the picturesque junction town of Guareiras, where an elevated wooden control tower looks down on tracks going in five directions, with semaphores showing which trains will stop by the vintage station and freight house. In addition to FCC traffic, nearby sugar mills sometimes send steam powered cane trains through here, and there is also a local rail-bus service.

## Havana to Pinar del Rio

| Reg. frt. 1131 | Psgr. 103 | Psgr. 101 | Station | Km. | Psgr. 102 | Psgr. 104 | Frt. 1132 |
|---|---|---|---|---|---|---|---|
| 23:25 | 15:42 | 22:45 | Havana | 0.0 | 06:05 | 14:43 | 05:20 |
| 01:26 | 17:00 | 23:56 | Rincon | 24.1 | 04:44 | 13:18 | 03:29 |
| 06:31 | 19:55 | 02:37 | Taco Taco | 112.2 | 01:55 | 10:23 | 21:59 |
| 09:20 | 21:05 | 03:43 | Herradura | 146.6 | 00:47 | 09:15 | 18:37 |
| 11:05 | 22:06 | 04:40 | Pinar del Rio | 17.79 | 23:50 | 08:15 | 17:00 |

Two trains in each direction provide passenger service from Havana west to Pinar del Rio, which has a hotel near the station.

## Havana to Cienfuegos

| 7 | 11 | 17 | | | 18 | 12 | 8 |
|---|---|---|---|---|---|---|---|
| 09:20 | 10:15 | 14:20 | Havana | 00 | 11:23 | 06:25 | 05:27 |
| 10:20 | 11:19 | 15:19 | Jaruco | 43:1 | 10:18 | 05:22 | 04:29 |
| 11:08 | 12:10 | 16:10 | Matanzas | 90.4 | 09:25 | 04:29 | 03:40 |
| 14:22 | | 19:27 | Santa Clara | 285.9 | 06:10 | | 00:25 |
| | 15:58 | | Cruces | | | 00.39 | |
| | 17:04 | | Cienfuegos | | | 23:30 | |

Mainline service from Havana eastward to Matanzas is provided by at least 3 trains each way in addition to the overnight expresses, thus allowing for connections with Hershey electric cars at Jaruco and at Matanzas for interesting round trips. Note that two of these trains continue on to Santa Clara, while the third goes to Cruces and Cienfuegos, passing several steam-powered sugar mills.

*Above: Cobblestones and horse drawn wagons grace the street side of Santa Clara's handsome station, on the FCC's national mainline.*
AHW Photo

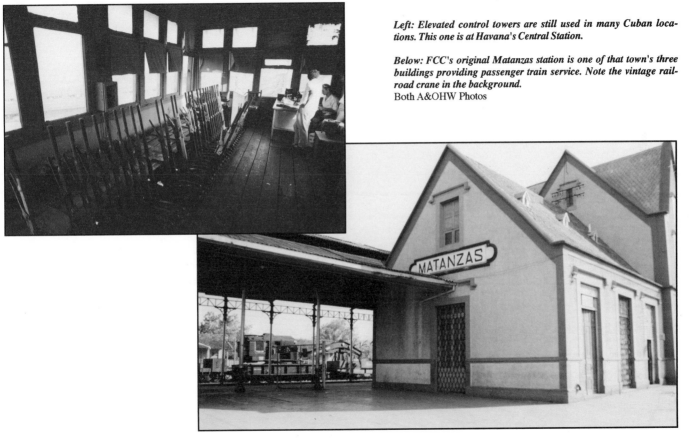

*Left: Elevated control towers are still used in many Cuban locations. This one is at Havana's Central Station.*

*Below: FCC's original Matanzas station is one of that town's three buildings providing passenger train service. Note the vintage railroad crane in the background.*
Both A&OHW Photos

# Hershey Electric

In addition to its impressive array of operating American steam locomotives and its unusual international collection of mainline diesels, Cuba also has the last old style American electric interurban system, complete with some of the original Brill cars for passengers and General Electric steeplecab engines for freight.

Connecting the capital Havana with the port city of Matanzas, this 57-mile mainline was originally known as the Hershey Cuban

Railway. Milton Hershey, the Pennsylvania chocolate tycoon, bought 35,000 acres of land in that area in 1916 to produce his own sugar, building a large sugar mill complete with American-style company town and a then-modern electric railroad. Although politics and owners have changed tremendously since that time, the whole operation continues today with only minimal alterations. The name Hershey was formally dropped after the Revolu-

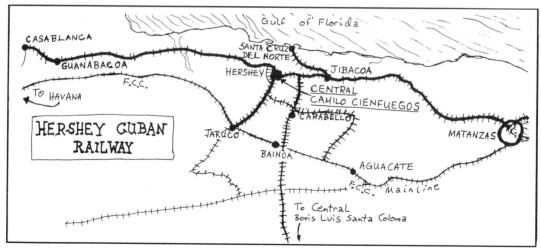

*Seventy-five years ago this scene would not have looked a whole lot different, although interurban car 3010 would still be nearly new, having come to Hershey from Brill at the end of the first world war. In this 1995 scene the car was waiting to make an afternoon run to the coastal town of Santa Cruz del Norte.*
A&OHW Photo

*Trains of Cuba*

tion, the mill and railroad both being renamed for revolutionary hero Camilo Cienfuegos. The company town however, along with the railroad station and locomotive shop, continues to be called Hershey. More recently the line has also become known as the Cuban Electric Railway (Ferrocarriles Electrico de Cuba), to differentiate it from the rest of Cuba's railway system (the dieselized FCC) of which it is officially a division.

Current operations offer eight daily interurban trains for passengers along the mainline (far less than the original hourly service), plus service on three shorter branchlines. An ambitious traveller could cover all this trackage in a single day by checking the schedules carefully. Joining a tour group would make this easiest and would probably include a visit to the Hershey shop, with its varied electric and diesel power under repair. Tour groups can travel the whole electric system aboard No. 3008, one of the original arch-roofed Brill interurban cars recently rebuilt by Hershey shop crews for charter service and proudly lettered "Trans Hershey" over its sleek red and white paint scheme. For variety, tour groups can also arrange a mixed train, with a GE steeplecab hauling freight cars along with one of the outside braced boxcars now outfitted as coaches with windows and seats.

Four daily passenger trains serve a branch line to the coastal town of Santa Cruz del Norte, usually with a pair of cars. Although Santa Cruz is just a couple of miles from Hershey, the train takes ten miles to get there, going a round about route between coastal hills that provides more people with the service.

An ambitious schedule of 12 trains daily provides service on another branch line ending at the pleasant town of Carabello, where the electric cars do a bit of street running. A round trip takes little more than an hour and is usually made by a single car.

Busiest, longest and newest of the three branch lines goes 12 miles to Jaruco. Built in 1931, it is scheduled for 14 round trips daily, more than half of them running at night. At Jaruco connections can be made from the mill and town at Hershey to FCC passenger trains for the rest of the country.

The Camilo Cienfuegos Division has total trackage of 181.8 miles (292.6 km) with 128.4 miles (206.6 km) being electrified. Perhaps most interesting among the latter is the freight-only trackage that leaves the Matanzas passenger terminal and wanders down back streets of the old city, then hugs the coastal bay on its way out to the port and warehouse area, where security restricts photographs. Electric locomotives service some acopios during the sugar season, as do several diesels on non-electrified trackage. The diesel fleet includes a few models from Baldwin, Alco and GE, but all these require American parts if they are to run again.

| Mainline Schedule | | | |
|---|---|---|---|
| Leave Casablanca (Havana) | Arrive Matanzas | Leave Matanzas | Arrive Casablanca |
| 04:10 | 08:03 | 04:00 | 07:57 |
| 10:20 | 14:06 | 10:00 | 13:42 |
| 14:55 | 18:48 | 14:56 | 18:48 |
| 21:10 | 00:46 | 21:00 | 00:36 |

*Branchline passenger service is still a frequent occurrence on the main street of Carabello, where we see interurban car No. 3020 with a nearly full load of passengers bound for Hershey, where connections will take them to Havana or Matanzas. This unit was converted to electric service by Hershey shop crews from an old American heavyweight coach.*
A&OHW Photo

# Hershey Electric Roster

| Interurban Cars | | Builder |
|---|---|---|
| 3006 | Arch roof | Brill |
| 3007 | " " | " |
| 3008 | " " | " |
| 3009 | " " | " |
| 3010 | " " | " |
| 3011 | " " | " |
| 3016 | " " | " |
| 3018 | Deck Roof | Converted from heavyweight coach at Hershey |
| 3019 | Flat Roof | " " |
| 3020 | " " | " " |
| 3021 | Deck | " " |
| 3022 | Streamline | Converted from West German rail-bus |
| 3023 | " | " " |
| 3024 | " | " " |
| 3025 | " | " " |
| 3026 | " | " " |
| 3027 | " | " " |
| 072 | Line car | Rebuilt from old equipment |
| 073 | " | " " |

| Electric Locomotives | | Builder | No. | Year | Original No. |
|---|---|---|---|---|---|
| 20801 | Steeple Cab | General Electric | 7689 | 1920 | 20 |
| 20802 | " " | " " | 7691 | " | 22 |
| 20803 | " " | " " | | " | |
| 20804 | " " | " " | 7694 | 1920 | 25 |
| 20806 | " " | " " | 9922 | 1925 | 27 |
| 20807 | " " | " " | 9923 | " | 28 |
| 20808 | " " | " " | 9924 | 1925 | 29 |
| 21001 | Modified | | | | |
| 21002 | " " | " " | 7692 | 1920 | 23 |
| 21004 | " " | " " | 10142 | 1926 | This car built as Havana Central Railway No. 459 |
| 21201 | " " | " " | | | |
| 21202 | Diesel Conversion | Brissoneau | | | |

*A slow day inside the large Hershey shops finds some of the workers taking a break inside interurban passenger car No. 3023, at left, which was converted to electric operation some years ago from a second-hand German railbus. Steeplecab No. 20808, on the right, has been hauling freight over this line for more than 70 years, having arrived here new from General Electric in 1925 as Hershey No. 29.*
AHW Photo, with Wildy

*Ready tracks look equally busy outside the Hershey shops, with a varied fleet of red painted equipment. GE steeplecab No. 20802 is one of the original electric freight locomotives, sent here when the line was new in 1920, at that time carrying the No. 22. Meeting its nose is the nose of No. 21202, a one-of-a-kind conversion from a French diesel to a Cuban electric locomotive. Line car 072 is next, with interurban passenger car 3018 at the right. Both these units also received major rebuilding over the years at the Hershey shops. Smokestacks in the background are from the old Hershey sugar mill, one of the country's largest, now named Central Camilo Cienfuegos.*
AHW Photo, with Wildy

*Trains of Cuba*

While the focus during visits to sugar mills is usually on steam locomotives, it should be noted that a lot of other interesting equipment is also being operated, and that the operators are usually friendly people performing traditional railroad tasks often not seen anymore at modern facilities elsewhere in the world. On these two pages are examples of interesting railroad details to watch for when making a study tour.

*Above: Link and pin couplers are still found in a few locations. This one was on a 30-inch gauge gondola in the yard at Central Pepito Tey.*

*Above Right: Auxiliary Car No. 01 stands ready for duty in the yard of Central Obdulio Morales, a 27 1/2-inch narrow gauge line powered by both steam and diesel. Painted a pleasing yellow with green trim, it brings tools, materials and workers to the sites of derailments or track problems.*

*Opposite, top: Central Simon Bolivar's narrow gauge caboose No. 1 is the model of simplicity, providing shelter and passage to crews at the tail end of their sugar trains. Track-side farmers often climb aboard as well, bringing bicycles, pigs and implements, seemingly oblivious to the dangers of riding these antique trains as they wobble over old, worn, narrow tracks without so much as train brakes or other safety devices. Railroad operations like these haven't been seen in North America since the early part of this century.*

*Opposite, bottom: Car frames, couplers and trucks came to Cuba from many manufacturers, mostly in the U.S.A. This unusual pair of archbar trucks with spoked wheels was on a caboose at Central Simon Bolivar, one of three mills using the equally unusual 27 1/2 inch gauge.*
AHW Photos

*Trains of Cuba*

*Trains of Cuba*

# ★ CUBAN STEAM ROSTER ★

The following pages provide information about active Cuban steam known to this author as of 1996. It is by no means a complete list of all steam engines in Cuba. Many other remaining engines are derelicts, with probably no future other than scrap. Most of these are not listed here, unless they are historically important. Some Cuban sugar mills still have their own original locomotives, though most have been involved in the engine swapping that has become especially easy and common since the Ministry of Sugar (Minaz) took over all mills in the country. Engine swapping makes listings such as the ones in this book difficult to maintain. For instance, an engine on a scrap line at one mill could well show up alive and working the next year at some other one. Among Cuba's large and varied steam fleet only a few are locomotives that came second hand from the U.S. Most were specifically ordered for Cuban service. However, many active sugar mill engines began their careers on one or the other of Cuba's former mainline railroads, especially Consolidations, Ten-Wheelers and Moguls, but also a couple of tankers that worked out of downtown Havana in the late 1890s. Most importantly, Cuba today operates the largest and most varied collection of early 1900s American motive power in the world.

Dieselization began at some sugar mills before the Revolution with American engines, but the bulk of sugar diesels came in the 1960's and 70's from Russia. These are generally painted orange and white, resemble first generation American diesels and can be found all over Cuba. The mills at the east end of the island are more thoroughly dieselized than those in the west. The plan had been to standard gauge all sugar mills and operate them with one or two classes of motive power. This goal is still expected to be reached with recently welcomed foreign investments in the sugar industry.

Mills that operate steam locomotives can often be spotted from miles away due to the dark plumes of smoke from fuel oil. Seeing such a plume in distant cane fields is an easy way to locate steam powered trains, though getting closer by road often becomes a major challenge. There are no tow trucks or public telephones in most rural areas, in case your rented car breaks down. No public washrooms or fast food places either, though lots of friendly people willing to help out with their oxen, bicycles, or even tractors.

Some rail historians have decried the attempts by Minaz at standardizing sugar mills since the Revolution, including their renaming (often for revolutionary heroes or martyrs) and the renumbering of all the locomotives. But changes are part of history; old struggling railroads don't own their operating practices to historians. Having all steam engines numbered in a single series certainly helps to keep track of them, otherwise the listings in this book alone would have several dozen engines each numbered one, two or three.

Roster experts with investigative leanings long tried to figure out the exact Minaz numbering system, which basically runs from 1101 to 1911. A rough generalization is that the greater a locomotive's tractive effort the higher its second number. For instance, No. 1101 is a 1907 Vulcan 0-6-0 saddle tanker, while No. 1911 is a 1925 Alco 2-8-2 that used to be in mainline service on the Cuba Railroad. Narrow gauge engines don't go above No. 1667.

Getting a bit more complex, locomotive numbers are also assigned according to the locations of their mills, with a western mill like Mal Tiempo having low third numbers like 1320 and eastern mills like Rafael Freyre with 1391. But this system is not fully reliable either, especially with the frequent swapping of engines.

The maps that accompany this section are composites made from the sketches and information gathered by several people. Dotted lines indicate dirt roads, which may be smooth and well-maintained or - especially in wet times - impassable. In all cases, it would be advisable to check out train routes and road conditions locally, or with train crews. Sugar mill railroads may change operations from one year to the next, especially regarding which reload points are served. Unused lines may lay abandoned for years then be reopened, or torn up, while new lines and branches continue to be built.

The most basic sugarcane reload is the ox-powered "chucho," which lifts bundles of fresh-cut cane from trucks, trailers and ox-carts, then lowers them directly into empty cane cars. A modernized variation uses diesel motors instead of oxen for the power. Operating chuchos are rare, having been mostly replaced by the "acopio." Here the cane is brought in from the fields and first chopped into shorter pieces, then loaded into cars with a conveyor belt which passes through an area of fans that blow off the leaves and "chaff," thus delivering a cleaner product in greater bulk to the mills. An even larger version of the acopio is called a "centro limpiesa."

## Two of Cuba's Very Oldest

1. In the main lobby of Havana's downtown railroad station sits the "La Junta," a standard gauge 4-2-2 built for the Matanzas Railway by Rogers in 1843. Back in the year 1900 this became Cuba's first preserved locomotive.

2. Cuba's oldest *operable* locomotive is Central R.M. Villena's coal-burning 0-4-2T No. 1112, built by Baldwin in 1878 and initially placed in public service between Regla and Casablanca. Later it did switching work for the sugar mill of Averoff, which was demolished in 1907 and replaced by the current Villena mill, at that time named Central Rosario.

*This recent photo of No. 1112 was taken near the Villena millyard. With coal scarce in Cuba, the engine is fired up mainly for visiting tour groups.*
Wildy Photo

## Roster Information is Listed as follows:
Mill number (from Ministry of Sugar); current mill name; original name (in parantheses); province; gauge;
locomotive number (Ministry of Sugar); wheel arrangment; builder; year built; construction number; additional data.

## 103 — Standard Gauge
### Eduardo Garcia Lavandero (El Pilar) La Habana

| | | | | | |
|---|---|---|---|---|---|
| 1302 | 2-6-0 | Alco | 1904 | 30235 | |
| 1504 | 4-6-0 | BLW | 1923 | 57010 | |
| 1704 | 2-8-0 | Vulcan | 1919 | 2893 | |
| 1705 | 2-8-0 | BLW | 1920 | 53147 | |

This mill also has an 0-4-0T, 2-6-0 and 2-8-0 on scrapline.

## 105 — Narrow Gauge, 3-foot
### Augusto Cesar Sandino (Mercedita) La Habana

| | | | | | |
|---|---|---|---|---|---|
| 2 | 2-6-0 | BLW | 1923 | 56920 | |
| 1114 | 2-6-0 | BLW | 1892 | 12998 | Dismantled; a classic. |
| 1209 | 2-6-0 | BLW | 1905 | 25214 | Built for this mill as No. 1. Last worked in1992. |
| 1210 | 2-6-0 | BLW | 1913 | 40595 | Worked for a time at Lenin Park in Havana, hauling kids and visitors as "No. 3." |
| 1350 | 2-8-0 | BLW | 1916 | 43394 | Built as No. 3 for Central San Jose, now Hermanos Ameijeiras. |
| 1382 | 2-8-0 | BLW | 1915 | 42690 | Built as Cuban Central RR No. 7. |
| 1404 | 2-8-0 | Alco | 1919 | 58746 | Built as Cuban Central RR No.18. |

| | | | | | |
|---|---|---|---|---|---|
| 1405 | 2-6-0 | Henschel | 1913 | 12429 | |
| 1424 | 2-8-0 | BLW | 1920 | 54233 | Derelict |

Closed during recent fuel shortages, the railroad has been rebuilt, locomotive repairs performed, then reopened as a short industrial operation (field trackage abandoned). One of three 3-foot gauge lines in Cuba still using steam.

## 107 — Standard Gauge
### Pablo de La Torriente Brau (Orozco) Pinar del Rio

| | | | | | |
|---|---|---|---|---|---|
| 1101 | 0-6-0ST | Vulcan | 1907 | 1177 | Built for this mill as No. 1. Now preserved on site. |
| 1102 | 2-6-0 | Vulcan | 1915 | 2421 | Built for this mill as No 2, named "Maria Josefa." |
| 1103 | 2-6-0 | BLW | 1920 | 54052 | Built for this mill as No. 5. |
| 1501 | 2-6-0 | Rogers | 1894 | 5000 | One of Cuba's oldest operating locomotives. Built as 2-6-4T Forney. |
| 1505 | 2-6-0 | BLW | 1910 | 35462 | |
| 1662 | 2-6-0 | Vulcan | 1920 | 3081 | |
| 1703 | 2-6-0 | Henschel | 1920 | 18029 | |

Among Cuba's biggest fleet of Moguls at one mill; the most varied collection, including a real antique, plus a German edition. Nice scenery, a photogenic bridge, some street running.

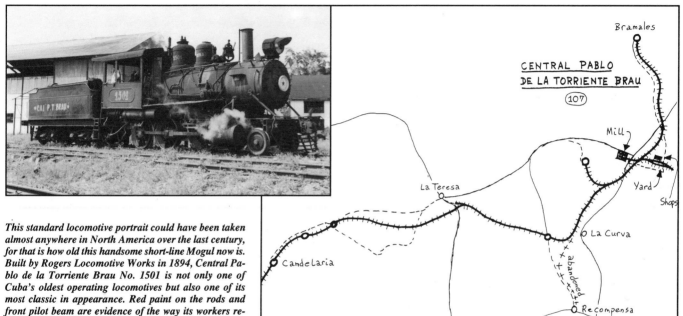

This standard locomotive portrait could have been taken almost anywhere in North America over the last century, for that is how old this handsome short-line Mogul now is. Built by Rogers Locomotive Works in 1894, Central Pablo de la Torriente Brau No. 1501 is not only one of Cuba's oldest operating locomotives but also one of its most classic in appearance. Red paint on the rods and front pilot beam are evidence of the way its workers respect this aged machine. The star on the front plate was a proud custom on short-lines of the past. Visitors to Cuba sometimes think the many stars painted everywhere represent a political party, but actually they've been on the Cuban flag since independence from Spain and serve as a popular national symbol. Behind No. 1501 is P.T. Brau's spacious locomotive shop.

AHW Photo

| 108 | | | | | Standard Gauge |
|---|---|---|---|---|---|
| Jose Marti (San Cristobal) Pinar del Rio | | | | | |
| 1401 | 2-6-0 | Alco | 1908 | 45659 | |
| 1502 | 2-8-0 | Vulcan | 1920 | 3090 | Built for this mill as No. 1. |
| 1701 | 2-8-0 | BLW | 1920 | 53802 | |
| 1702 | 2-8-0 | Vulcan | 1919 | 2999 | Built as Cuba Northern No. 40. |

*Trains of Cuba*

## 201                                   *Standard Gauge*
### Amistad con los Pueblos (Amistad) La Habana

| 1106 | 0-4-0ST | BLW | 1888 | 9683 | Preserved at Guines. |
| 1303 | 2-6-0 | Alco | 1905 | 38900 | Built for this mill as No. 4. |
| 1509 | 2-6-0 | Alco | 1910 | 49086 | |
| 1707 | 2-6-0 | BLW | 1920 | 53823 | |
| 1712 | 2-6-0 | Porter | 1916 | 5747 | |
| 1803 | 2-8-0 | BLW | 1919 | 52195 | |
| 1804 | 2-8-0 | BLW | 1919 | 52245 | |
| 1805 | 2-8-0 | BLW | 1920 | 52913 | |

The three Consolidations were built new for nearby Central Toledo (now Ctrl. Manuel Martinez Prieto) as Nos. 10, 11 and 12. Steam works east of mill and west on nearby FCC tracks, passing FCC station at Guines.

## 206                                   *Standard Gauge*
### Manuel Isla Perez (Josefita) La Habana

| 1107 | 0-4-2T | BLW | 1882 | 6468 | 2nd oldest running loco. in Cuba. |
| 1205 | 0-4-4T | Porter | 1905 | 3356 | |
| 1208 | 2-4-2T | Rogers | 1894 | 5007 | Built for United Railways of Havana, named "Margarita y Teresa." Derelict. |
| 1603 | 2-8-0 | Alco | 1925 | 65194 | |
| 1708 | 2-8-0 | BLW | 1920 | 54227 | |
| 1802 | 2-8-0 | Porter | 1917 | 6053 | |

Line work is not too interesting, but the three tankers that take turns switching the mill yard certainly are. The switcher usually comes out of mill area on line east two or three times an hour to pick up more loads, which allows some limited photography. Larger engines serve reload beyond mill, plus a branch to the south-east.

*Above: Central Manuel Isla Perez has a trio of tankers that includes this 1905 Porter 0-4-4T pushing a load of cane towards the sugar mill's unloading dock.*
AHW Photo

## 207
## Gregorio Arlee Manalich (Mercedita) La Habana

Narrow Gauge

| | | | | | |
|---|---|---|---|---|---|
| 5 | 0-6-0 ST | MW & Co. England | 1873 | | A historic treaure but very decrepit condition. Built for Bay of Havana RR and named "Guamacaro." |
| 1305 | 2-6-0 | Vulcan | 1916 | 2492 | Another rare locomotive, now derelict. |
| 1306 | 2-8-0 | BLW | 1912 | 38802 | |
| 1307 | 2-8-0 | BLW | 1920 | 53685 | Built new for this mill as No. 2. |
| 1308 | 2-8-0 | BLW | 1900 | 18371 | |
| 1338 | 2-6-0 | BLW | 1920 | 53339 | Yard switcher |
| 1351 | 2-8-0 | BLW | 1917 | 45070 | Built as 3-foot gauge Ctrl. Hermanos Ameijeiras No. 4 Changed here in '92. |
| 1365 | 2-8-0 | BLW | 1924 | 57791 | |

Standard Gauge

| | | | | | |
|---|---|---|---|---|---|
| 1304 | 2-8-0 | Vulcan | 1918 | 2792 | |
| 1402 | 2-6-0 | BLW | 1918 | 52514 | |
| 1403 | 2-6-0 | Rogers | 1892 | 4647 | Another antique, still working. |
| 1709 | 0-6-0T | BLW | 1907 | 29986 | Classic tanker, but decrepit. Built as United Railways of Havana No. P14. |

A large, impressive mill and adjacent dual-gauge locomotive shop. Road trains and mill switchers pass through a photogenic stone walled gate to reach the yard area. At a nearby diamond junction the standard gauge FCC crosses the 2'6" sugar line. Inbound loads battle a steep grade up to the junction, which is controlled by a homemade semaphore signal. A quaint FCC station is just down the track. Although this mill relies almost totally on steam power, the site is ironically a provincial diesel centre for the Ministry of Sugar.

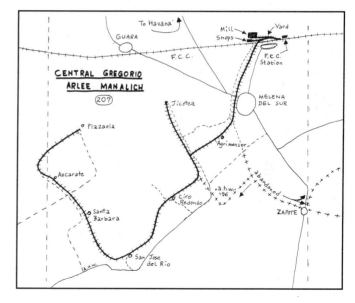

## 210

*Narrow (30") & Standard Gauge*

### Osvaldo Sanchez (Providencia) La Habana

Narrow Gauge

| 1110 | 2-8-0 | BLW | 1920 | 53402 | Built new for this mill as No. 6. |
|------|-------|-----|------|-------|------------------------------------|
| 1309 | 2-8-0 | Alco | | | |
| 1310 | 2-8-0 | BLW | 1919 | 52574 | |
| 1347 | 2-8-0 | BLW | 1919 | 52262 | |
| 1364 | 2-8-0 | BLW | 1912 | 37822 | |

Standard Gauge

| 1204 | 2-4-2T | Rogers | 1894 | 5009 | Built as United Railways of Havana "Providenzia." Another valuable antique. |
|------|--------|--------|------|------|------------------------------------|
| 1507 | 2-6-0 | Alco | 1912 | 52036 | |

A short drive from mill 207. Going back and forth every few hours between them can produce a variety of activity and locomotives. An early gas loco switches the standard gauge trackage, along with the rare Rogers 2-4-2T which was recently converted from coal back to oil ( less difficult to obtain). The narrow gauge serves several reloads on a relatively straight 10 kms of track south of the mill. A dirt road right next to the tracks, allows some exciting pacing. Also runs 2 kms. east of mill.

## 211

*Standard Gauge*

### Ruben Martinez Villena (Rosario) La Habana

| 1112 | 0-4-2T | BLW | 1878 | 4502 | Built as FC Ibanez No. 1. Cuba's oldest operating locomotive! |
|------|--------|-----|------|------|------------------------------------|
| 1201 | 0-4-2ST | Vulcan | 1916 | 2578 | |
| 1206 | 0-4-0T | Henschel | 1920 | 18044 | Derelict |
| 1207 | 2-4-0T | Henschel | 1912 | 11677 | Coal burning |
| 1311 | 2-6-2T | BLW | 1904 | 24839 | Built for neighboring mill Osvaldo Sanchez as Central Providencia No. 1. |

| 1411 | 2-6-0 | BLW | 1916 | 44919 | Built as 0-6-0 |
|------|-------|-----|------|-------|------------------------------------|
| 1508 | 2-8-0 | BLW | 1906 | 29616 | Built as Cuban Central RR No.104. |
| 1602 | 2-8-0 | BLW | 1920 | 54229 | |
| 1605 | 2-8-0 | BLW | 1920 | 54051 | |

This mill is sort of a mate to Manuel Isla Perez (206) in that these two operate the most interesting and historic fleet of tank engines. Line runs west to an interlocking tower, then north to reload. This was formerly a Hershey mill.

## 212

*Standard Gauge*

### Boris Luis Santa Coloma (San Antonio) La Habana

| 1510 | 2-6-0 | Alco | 1907 | 44702 | |
|------|-------|------|------|-------|------------------------------------|
| 1511 | 2-6-0 | Alco | 1912 | 52035 | |
| 1512 | 2-6-0 | Alco | 1917 | 56995 | Built for this mill as No. 5. |
| 1604 | 2-6-0 | BLW | 1920 | 53822 | |
| 1606 | 2-6-0 | Vulcan | 1920 | 3143 | |
| 1711 | 2-8-0 | Alco | 1920 | 62099 | Built for this mill as No. 1. |
| 1806 | 2-8-0 | Vulcan | 1918 | 2898 | |

Another mill formerly belonging to Hershey Chocolate. Husky, hard-working engines. Steam regularly switches freight cars from FCC tracks. One of the few mills willing to assign steam doubleheaders to heavy trains. Grinds extra cane when nearby mill 211 is not working, the two often exchanging cars at a diamond crossing guarded by genuine elevated tower and signals. Line runs north from mill; also east, skirting south edge of the town of Madruga. Trains usually make a good show charging into mill.

*Trains of Cuba*

**38**

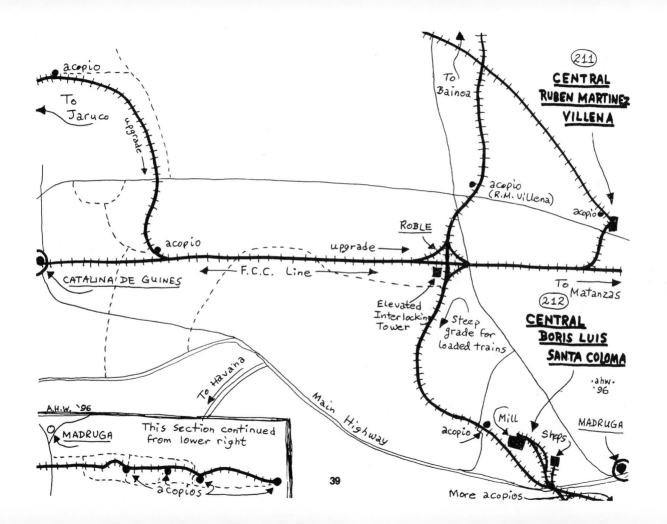

acopio

To Jaruco

upgrade

acopio

CATALINA DE GUINES

To Bainoa

(211)
**CENTRAL
RUBEN MARTINEZ
VILLENA**

acopio
(R.M. Villena)

acopio

ROBLE

upgrade →

← F.C.C. Line →

To Matanzas →

Elevated
Interlocking
Tower

Steep
grade for
loaded trains

(212)
**CENTRAL
BORIS LUIS
SANTA COLOMA**

.ahw.
'96

MADRUGA

acopio

Mill

Shops

To Havana

Main Highway

A.H.W. '96

MADRUGA

This section continued
from lower right

acopios

More acopios

39

## 302

### Reynold Garcia (Araujo) Matanzas — *Standard Gauge*

| | | | | |
|---|---|---|---|---|
| 1408 | 2-6-0 | Vulcan | 1918 | 2787 |
| 1517 | 2-6-0 | BLW | 1907 | 32083 |
| 1518 | 2-6-0 | Vulcan | 1916 | 2566 |

**Short operation that sees some diesel work.**

## 303

### Australia (Australia) Matanzas — *Standard Gauge*

| | | | | | |
|---|---|---|---|---|---|
| 1513 | 2-8-0 | BLW | 1920 | 54067 | |
| 1515 | 4-6-0 | Alco | 1914 | 54844 | Built as Havana Central RR No. 73. |
| 1593 | 2-6-0 | BLW | 1915 | 42299 | Built for this mill and named "Antonio Alvarez." |
| 1607 | 2-6-0 | BLW | 1920 | 52789 | |

| | | | | |
|---|---|---|---|---|
| 1613 | 2-6-0 | BLW | | |
| 1620 | 2-6-0 | Henschel | 1920 | 18030 |
| 1716 | 2-6-0 | Henschel | 1913 | 12428 |

## 304

### Granma (Carolina) Matanzas — *Standard Gauge*

| | | | | | |
|---|---|---|---|---|---|
| 1519 | 2-8-0 | Alco | 1916 | 56660 | Built as United Railways of Havana No. 112 - derelict. |
| 1713 | 2-8-0 | BLW | 1925 | 58486 | |
| 1714 | 2-8-0 | BLW | 1920 | 54139 | |
| 1812 | 2-8-0 | BLW | 1919 | 52488 | Built as Cuba RR No. 312. One of two largest 2-8-0's in Cuba. |

**A busy operation, but not particularly photogenic. One engine works the mill yard and big, new reload right next door. Another engine makes the long run to a reload north of the town of Carlos Rojas. While empties are being loaded, this engine comes back with its caboose and parks at the old FCC station in Carlos Rojas, offering an unusual photo. It also takes water from the old standpipe there. Later it highballs past the station with its loaded train, trailing a cloud of black smoke. Engines here are generally grimy. Has small gas locomotives to switch mill. Sometimes exchanges locomotives and cane with neighboring Central Victoria de Yaguajay. Line runs south-east to town of Jovellanos, then to a reload about one mile north of town of Carlos Rojas. Loaded train often meets an empty at Jovellanos.**

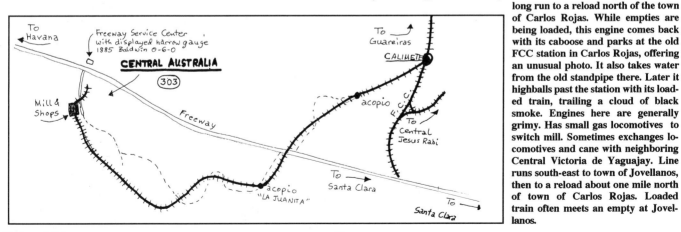

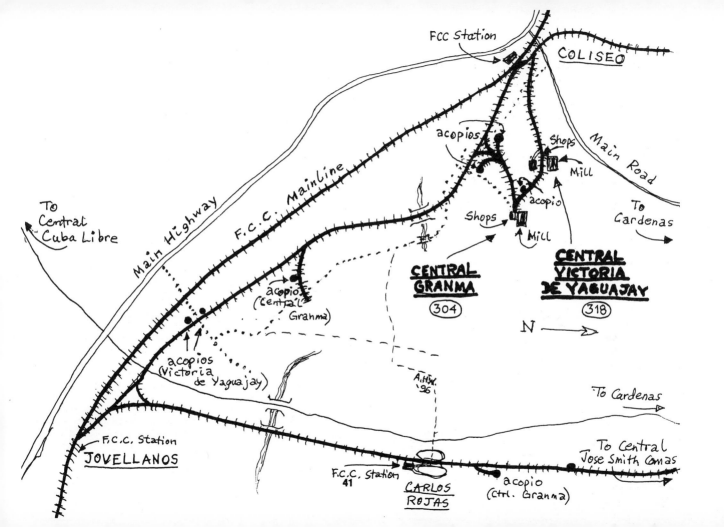

## 305                 *Standard Gauge*
### Puerto Rico Libre (Conchita) Matanzas

| 1409 | 2-6-0 | Henschel | 1913 | 12373 | |
|------|-------|----------|------|-------|--|
| 1527 | 2-6-2 | Alco | | | |
| 1609 | 2-6-0 | Vulcan | 1913 | 2080 | |
| 1718 | 2-8-0 | BLW | 1920 | 54286 | Overhaul |
| 1901 | 2-8-0 | BLW | 1919 | 52567 | Built as Cuba RR No. 322. One of two largest 2-8-0's in Cuba. |

## 306
### Cuba Libre (Cuba) Matanzas        *Standard Gauge*

| 1410 | 2-6-0 | Vulcan | 1916 | 2573 | |
|------|-------|--------|------|------|--|
| 1520 | 2-6-0 | Vulcan | 1920 | 3079 | |
| 1610 | 2-6-0 | BLW | 1925 | 58800 | Built for this mill as No. 1. |
| 1611 | 2-6-0 | BLW | 1925 | 58801 | Built for this mill as No. 2. |
| 1612 | 2-6-0 | BLW | 1925 | 58802 | Built for this mill as No. 3. |
| 1808 | 2-6-0 | BLW | 1927 | 60212 | Built for this mill as No. 8. |

Trains run south, north-east and west from mill, but tracks are hard to follow by car. By one side of the mill is a road with buggy traffic, guarded by a hand-operated crossing gate with shanty, while on the other side of the mill is a classic little dispatcher's station marked "Oficina de Trafico," where all trains pass and the local folks like to hang out. A big 1920s car is sometimes seen cruising the area.

## 308             *Narrow Gauge (30")*
### Humberto Alvarez (Dos Rosas) Matanzas

| 1213 | 2-6-0 | BLW | 1920 | 53006 | |
|------|-------|----------|------|-------|--|
| 1242 | 2-8-0 | BLW | 1925 | 58791 | |
| 1315 | 2-8-0 | BLW | 1905 | 26193 | |
| 1356 | 2-8-0 | Vulcan | 1916 | 2571 | |
| 2309 | Bo-Bo | Atlas | 1938 | 2067 | Originally worked in Hawaii. |
| 14 | 4WD | Whitcomb | 1937 | 60001 | First diesel made by Whitcomb. |

This mill has been shut down for several years and may not reopen. Listed here because it is only 10 minutes from the tourist resort of Varadero and _may_ offer future excursion services. Its two small diesels are themselves historic and fairly rare. Has some 10 km of track with curves and grades.

*Opposite Page: Central Cuba Libre No. 1611 is one of three sister Moguls, built new for this mill by Baldwin in 1925, arriving here as Central Cuba No. 2. In this picture the engine has stopped at Mile Zero to get instructions from the yardmaster, who works in the "Oficina de Trafico" inside the fenced yard at left. The sugar mill itself is in the background, black smoke rising from both chimneys indicating that the machinery is at work. No smoke usually means the mill is shut down, either for repairs or lack of sugar to grind. The latter happens during heavy rains, when cane cutting machinery gets bogged down out in the fields.*
IHW Photo

## Fructuoso Rodriguez (Limones) Matanzas

| | | | | | |
|---|---|---|---|---|---|
| 1216 | 2-4-0 | Rogers | 1895 | 5036 | Built as a 2-4-4T Forney for United Railways of Havana and named "San Augustin." |
| 1313 | 2-6-2T | Alco | 1915 | 55282 | |
| 1526 | 4-6-0 | BLW | 1918 | 50996 | |
| 1594 | 2-8-0 | Alco | | | Ex-FCC No. 10501 |
| 1849 | 2-8-0 | BLW | 1920 | 53693 | |

A friendly mill, not far from the beaches of Varadero, with a fabulous antique in the form of an 1895 Rogers 2-4-0 No. 1216 which can be seen slipping and sliding on the grades in the yard almost daily. Diesels do most of the line work, though steam serves a couple of nearby reloads. Has a classic "American Shortline" kind of roster, including a yellow wooden caboose. There is a picturesque shop interior, partly open, with two tracks. Line runs about 4 miles south of mill; also west, and north to Limonar.

*Right: The face of an old timer - Central Fructuoso Rodriguez relies on this antique for regular mill switching, though most of its line work is now handled by diesels. Rogers built 2-4-0 No. 1216 back in 1895.*
AHW Photo

*Opposite Page: Recalling locomotive shops on short-lines throughout North America in the first half of the 20th century, Central Fructuoso Rodriguez presents a typical roster that includes 4-6-0 Ten-Wheeler No. 1526 - in for a boiler wash - along with Sierra look-alike Baldwin 2-8-0 No. 1849 and No. 1313, an Alco 2-6-2 tanker to switch the yard.*
A&IHW Photo

**314**

**Jesus Rabi (Porfuerza) Matanzas**

| | | | | | |
|---|---|---|---|---|---|
| 1413 | 2-6-0 | Cooke | 1891 | 2114 | *Standard Gauge* Built as Evansville & Terre Haute No. 50. |
| 1414 | 2-8-0 | Alco | 1920 | 622621 | |
| 1529 | 2-8-0 | BLW | 1912 | 38095 | |
| 1810 | 2-8-0 | Vulcan | 1920 | 3088 | Built as Comoa Quarry No. 17 |

*Above: Former Southern Railroad Mogul, Cuba's oldest road locomotive, which was No. 2100 on the Louisville, Evansville & St. Louis RR, then became Augusta Southern No. 21, Georgia & Florida No. 21, and finally to Cuba as La Paz Sugar Co. No. 4. Seen here in the Jesus Rabi shops while being completely rebuilt in 1996!*

AHW Photo

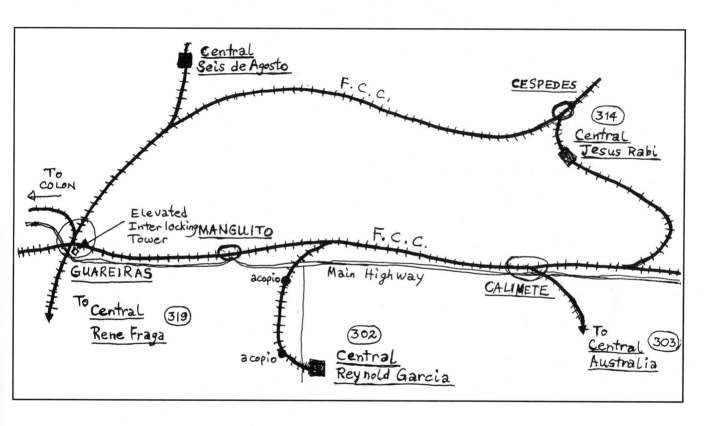

Central
Seis de Agosto

F. C. C.

CESPEDES

314

Central
Jesus Rabi

To
COLON

Elevated
Interlocking
Tower

MANGUITO

F. C. C.

GUAREIRAS

Main Highway

CALIMETE

acopio

To Central
Rene Fraga

319

302

Central
Reynold Garcia

acopio

To
Central
Australia

303

47

## 315                          *Standard Gauge*
### Jose Smith Comas (Progreso) Matanzas

| | | | | | |
|---|---|---|---|---|---|
| 1211 | 0-4-0ST | Vulcan | 1919 | 2961 | |
| 1122 | 0-4-0T | Porter | 1909 | 4437 | |
| 1406 | 2-6-0 | BLW | 1920 | EO151 | Derelict |
| 1415 | 2-6-0 | Vulcan | 1920 | 3075 | |
| 1530 | 2-6-0 | BLW | 1925 | 58654 | Built new for this mill as No. 1. |
| 1531 | 2-6-0 | BLW | 1925 | 58655 | Built new for this mill as No. 2. |
| 1715 | 0-6-0T | Alcos Brooks | 1916 | 56714 | Built as Havana Central RR No. P 25. Derelict. |

This is often the first mill visited by tourists and one of the favorites because it's just 20 minutes down the highway from Varadero. One or more of the Moguls does the line pickups, using FCC tracks and passing the FCC stations of Progreso and Contreras. The pair of sister Moguls came here new and are maintained in superb condition. No. 1406 was originally a Belgian-built locomotive, with only the boiler coming from Baldwin as extra order in 1920.

## 318                          *Standard Gauge*
### Victoria de Yaguajay (Santa Amelia) Matanzas

| | | | | | |
|---|---|---|---|---|---|
| 1514 | 2-8-0 | Alco | 1920 | 62508 | |
| 1533 | 4-6-0 | BLW | 1906 | 29392 | Built as Cuba RR No. 45. Derelict. |
| 1594 | 2-8-0 | Alco | --- | --- | Ex-FCC No. 10501. |
| 1614 | 2-8-0 | Vulcan | 1916 | 2448 | |
| 1811 | 2-8-0 | Vulcan | 1920 | 3144 | |
| 1813 | 2-8-0 | BLW | 1920 | 54138 | |

One of several basic, hard-working operations with minimal photogenic opportunities. Perhaps the best comes whenever a loaded train from the fields pulls through the little picturesque town of Coliseo on the FCC's mainline, before backing into the nearby millyard. Also, uses small 4-wheeled diesels, including one built by Vulcan Iron Works. Trackage in the cane fields is only accessible by rough roads; location of train can be seen for miles across the flat land from moving smoke plumes.

## 319                          *Standard Gauge*
### Rene Fraga (Santa Rita) Matanzas

| | | | | | |
|---|---|---|---|---|---|
| 1119 | 0-4-0T | Henschel | 1913 | 12496 | Derelict |
| 1524 | 2-6-2T | Porter | 1915 | 5741 | |
| 1532 | 2-6-0 | BLW | 1920 | 53918 | |
| 1618 | 2-8-0 | BLW | 1920 | 54100 | Built for this mill as No. 6. |
| 1719 | 2-8-0 | BLW | 1917 | | |
| 1723 | 2-8-0 | Alco | | | Derelict |
| 1820 | 2-8-0 | BLW | 1920 | 52969 | Recently arrived from Central George Washington. |

Some trains into cane fields are diesel hauled, but steam is usually used for work closer to the mill.

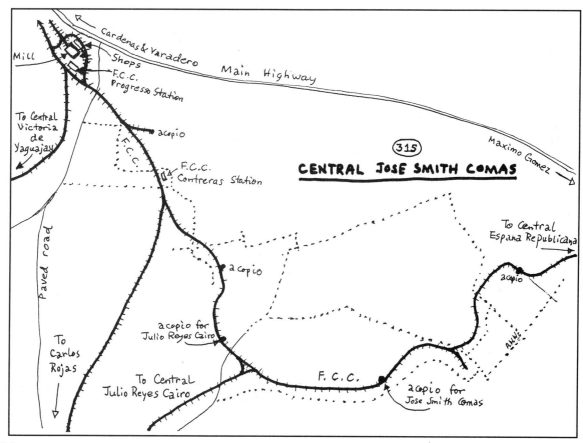

Mill

Cardenas & Varadero Main Highway

Shops
F.C.C. Progreso Station

315

CENTRAL JOSE SMITH COMAS

To Central Victoria de Yaguajay

F.C.C.

acopio

F.C.C. Contreras Station

Maximo Gomez

To Central Espana Republicana

acopio

Paved road

acopio

acopio

LINE

acopio for Julio Reyes Cairo

To Carlos Rojas

To Central Julio Reyes Cairo

F. C. C.

acopio for Jose Smith Comas

**320**                                    *Standard Gauge*

**Juan Avila (Santa Domingo)**

| 1534 | 4-6-0 | Baldwin | 1906 | 29391 | Built as Cuba RR No. 44. Derelict. |
| 1535 | 4-6-0 | Baldwin | 1906 | 29115 | Built as Cuba RR No. 41. |
| 1720 | 2-6-0 | Vulcan | 1920 | 3138 | |
| 1721 | 2-6-0 | Vulcan | 1920 | 3136 | |
| 1807 | 2-8-0 | Baldwin | 1916 | 44461 | |
| 1814 | 2-8-0 | Alco | 1919 | 60539 | Built as Havana Central RR No 268 |

**Also handles cane from Central Fructoso Rodriguez when that mill's not working. Line runs from mill west to Juan Gilberto Gomez and can be followed by road. Loaded trains have to double or triple a grade near end of the line.**

**321**                                    *Standard Gauge*

**Julio Reyes Cairo (Soledad)**

| 1123 | 0-6-0T | Borsig | 1910 | 7619 | |
| 1124 | 2-4-0T | Henschel | 1913 | 12445 | Coal burning |
| 1416 | 2-6-0 | BLW | 1924 | E0862 | Derelict |
| 1619 | 2-6-0 | Alco | 1915 | 55281 | |
| 1646 | 2-8-0 | BLW | 1920 | 54225 | |
| 1722 | 2-8-0 | BLW | 1891 | 12317 | Built as Buffalo, Rochester & Pittsburgh No. 53. Derelict. |

**Photogenic mill, town and railroad setting. A rare piece of American history is represented by the 1891 Baldwin No 1722, which is unfortunately in poor condition at this time.**

*Opposite: While Cuban sugar mills usually present scenes of vintage American railroading, Central Julio Reyes Cairo looks more like rural Europe sometime between the world wars. The setting itself is quite plain and industrial, a Czechoslovakian motorcycle with sidecar parked at the curb and a Russian truck rumbling down the main street. Switching the millyard is 0-6-0 tanker No. 1123, built in Germany by Borsig in 1910, and thus one of the few non-American steam locomotives operating in Cuba.*
IHW Photo

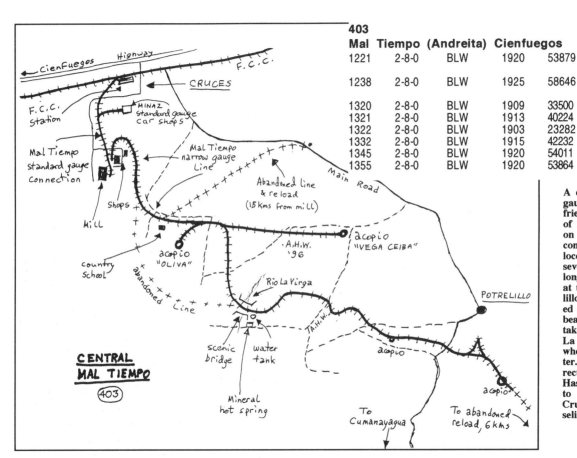

**CENTRAL MAL TIEMPO**

(403)

| 403 | | | | | Narrow Gauge (30") |
|---|---|---|---|---|---|
| **Mal Tiempo (Andreita) Cienfuegos** | | | | | |
| 1221 | 2-8-0 | BLW | 1920 | 53879 | Built new for this mill as No. 7. |
| 1238 | 2-8-0 | BLW | 1925 | 58646 | Derelict, though the line's newest engine! |
| 1320 | 2-8-0 | BLW | 1909 | 33500 | |
| 1321 | 2-8-0 | BLW | 1913 | 40224 | |
| 1322 | 2-8-0 | BLW | 1903 | 23282 | Complete overhaul. |
| 1332 | 2-8-0 | BLW | 1915 | 42232 | |
| 1345 | 2-8-0 | BLW | 1920 | 54011 | |
| 1355 | 2-8-0 | BLW | 1920 | 53864 | |

A classic all-steam narrow gauge operation, with very friendly people. Still has one of its original locomotives on stand-by duty. Has just completely rebuilt another locomotive with parts from several defunct mills. One long mainline to the reload at the farm town of Potrelillo, plus two reloads located on short branchlines. A beautiful old stone bridge takes the tracks across Rio La Virga, about midway, where engines stop for water. Rough roads, not direct, and impassible in rain. Has standard gauge track to the FCC at nearby Cruces, but this is now dieselized.

*Central Mal Tiempo has long been known for its friendly crews and interesting train operations, with over 20 kms of winding narrow gauge mainline track, plus spurs into some of the cane reloads. A fleet of well-kept 2-8-0's does the sugar hauling, all of them built by Baldwin between 1903 and 1920, when the current mill machinery was also new, having replaced a much older factory. In this yard scene No. 1345 is pushing a loaded train and its caboose toward the mill while No. 1355 gets ready to head out with a train of empties. Locomotive and car shops are off to the left.*
IHW Photo

**404**                       *Standard Gauge*

## Ciudad Caracas (Caracas) Cienfuegos

| 1538 | 2-6-2 | BLW | 1920 | 54230 | Built new for this mill as No. 2 |
|------|-------|-----|------|-------|----------------------------------|
| 1621 | 2-8-0 | Alco | 1924 | 65192 | |
| 1630 | 2-6-0 | Alco | 1920 | 62097 | |
| 1724 | 2-8-0 | BLW | 1920 | 53726 | Built new for this mill as No. 1 |
| 1725 | 2-6-0 | Alco | 1920 | 62098 | |

This mill is basically dieselized, but steam switches the yard and serves as backup.

**405**                       *Standard Gauge*

## Luis Arcos Bergnes (Carmita) Villa Clara

| 1539 | 2-6-0 | BLW | 1920 | 53704 |
|------|-------|-----|------|-------|
| 1541 | 2-6-0 | Alco | | |
| 1622 | 2-8-0 | BLW | 1923 | 57403 |
| 1755 | 2-8-0 | BLW | 1917 | 46533 |

Mill has been shut during some recent harvests. Located west of highway between Santa Clara and Caibarien.

**407**                       *Standard Gauge*

## Abel Santamaria (Constancia) Villa Clara

| 1425 | 2-6-0 | BLW | 1919 | 52341 |
|------|-------|-----|------|-------|

Mill basically dieselized, but still works on steam. Also has a displayed narrow gauge 2-6-0.

**408**                       *Standard Gauge*

## Mariana Grajales (Corazon de Jesus) Villa Clara

| 1224 | 2-4-0 | BLW | 1925 | 58438 | Undergoing repairs. |
|------|-------|-----|------|-------|---------------------|
| 1540 | 2-6-0 | BLW | 1924 | 58133 | Derelict |

**409**                       *Standard Gauge*

## Antonio Sanchez (Covadonga) Cienfuegos

| 1623 | 2-8-0 | BLW | 1920 | 53799 |
|------|-------|-----|------|-------|
| 1624 | 2-8-0 | BLW | 1916 | 44223 |
| 1625 | 2-8-0 | BLW | 1920 | 54054 |
| 1629 | 2-8-0 | BLW | 1920 | 6624115 |
| 1726 | 2-8-0 | Vulcan | 1920 | 3122 |

Some diesel, but uses mainly steam. Cane sometimes brought to neighboring Central Primero de Mayo.

**412**                       *Standard Gauge*

## Juan Pedro Carbo Servia (Fidencia) Villa Clara

| 1427 | 2-6-0 | Alco | 1922 | 62716 |
|------|-------|-----|------|-------|
| 1727 | 2-8-0 | BLW | 1920 | 53148 |
| 1728 | 2-8-0 | Vulcan | 19920 | 3114 | Major overhaul |

Railroad is dieselized, but uses steam to switch mill yard. Also has 4 derelicts, including a large Vulcan 0-4-0ST

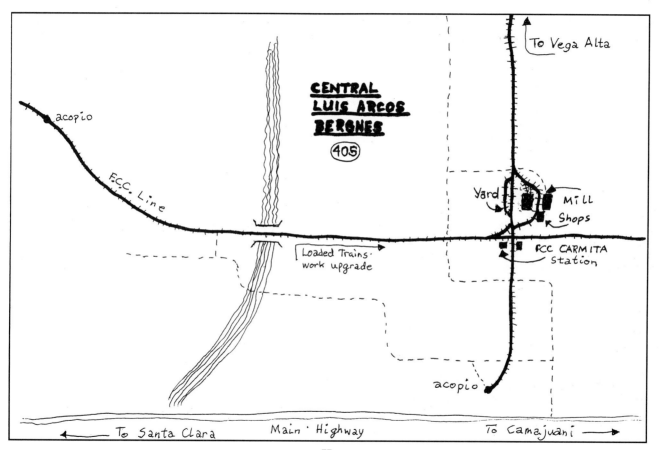

acopio

F.C.C. Line

CENTRAL
LUIS ARCOS
BERGNES
(405)

To Vega Alta

Yard

MiLL
Shops

Loaded Trains·
work upgrade

FCC CARMITA
Station

acopio

To Santa Clara    Main · Highway    To Camajuani

**55**

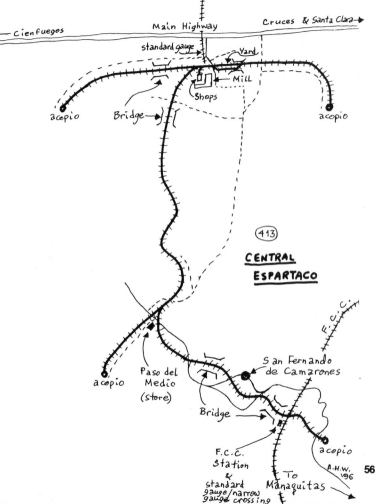

← Cienfuegos

Main Highway

Cruces & Santa Clara →

standard gauge

Yard

Mill

Shops

Bridge →

acopio

acopio

413

CENTRAL ESPARTACO

acopio

Paso del Medio (store)

Bridge

San Fernando de Camarones

F.C.C.

acopio

F.C.C. Station & standard gauge/narrow gauge crossing

To Manaquitas

A.H.W. 196

## 413                                              *Narrow Gauge (30")*
## Espartaco (Hormiguero) Cienfuegos

| | | | | | |
|---|---|---|---|---|---|
| 1130 | 0-4-0F | Orenstein & Koppel | 1914 | 6854 | Built for this mill as No 0. |
| 1131 | 0-4-0F | BLW | 1916 | 43277 | Built for this mill as No 00. |
| 1326 | 2-8-0 | BLW | 1895 | 14436 | Built for this mill as No 4. Oldest narrow gauge locomotive in regular service. |
| 1327 | 2-8-0 | BLW | 1911 | 37142 | Built for this mill as No 6. |
| 1328 | 2-8-0 | BLW | 1915 | 42093 | Built for this mill as No 7. |
| 1329 | 2-8-0 | BLW | 1919 | 52573 | Built for this mill as No 8. |
| 4123 | 4WD | Brookville | 1930's | 3451 | A classic 12-tonner |

One of the finest collections of original locomotives at any Cuban mill. A neighbor of Central Mal Tiempo. Has tracks to reloads going in both directions from the mill, plus a branchline with good bridges. Locomotives still assigned to individual crews. Two fireless 0-4-0's switch the yard, along with an aged, rickety Brookville gas engine. Another rare sight is the 12-seat narrow gauge railbus, built long ago by local crews, painted orange, and used to bring workers to the mill. Even more rare is its back-up, a little round roofed coach painted blue and hauled by the gas engine when needed. There is a bridge in the middle of the yard from where some of the mill action can be photographed. The century-old No. 1326 keeps busy right alongside the others. Locomotives are well kept at this mill, usually with brass domes and boiler bands shining. Also of note is that this mill's original No. 1, an 1884 Porter 0-4-2T is preserved at a park in nearby Cienfuegos. In 1996 the mill rebuilt an old 2-4-0 into a gas-mechanical locomotive to haul the coach on a more regular basis.

Another of Cuba's centenarians, Central Espartaco's 30-inch gauge Consolidation No. 1326 was sent to this mill by Baldwin in 1895, lettered Central Hormiguero No. 4. In this scene it was crossing a small creek while taking empties upgrade on a short line south of the mill. Espartaco has three more 2-8-0's, all built by Baldwin for this line and maintained in good condition.
IHW Photo

*Narrow Gauge (27 1/2")*

## Obdulio Morales (Narcisa) Sancti Spiritus

| 1137 | 2-6-0 | Baldwin | 1918 | 49555 | Built as Caibarien & Moron Ry. 0-6-0 No. 13. Now derelict. |
|------|-------|---------|------|-------|---|
| 1227 | 2-6-0 | Baldwin | 1892 | 13080 | Built for 30-inch gauge Central Triunvira. Derelict. |
| 1333 | 2-8-0 | Baldwin | 1919 | 52414 | Built as C&M No. 16. Also named "Pedro Pablo," and later "Camilo Cienfuegos." |
| 1334 | 2-8-0 | Baldwin | 1920 | 53655 | Built as C & M No. 17. Named "Don Alvaro," and later "Joaquin Paneca." |
| 1335 | 2-8-0 | Baldwin | 1905 | 26253 | Derelict - built for this line as No.5 |
| 1336 | 2-8-0 | Vulcan | 1918 | 2782 | Built as C&M No. 10. Named "Perlita," and later "Frank Pais." |
| 1354 | 2-8-0 | Baldwin | 1921 | 55127 | Built as 31 1/2" gauge Central Esperanza No. 8, (near Guantanamo), then to Central Diez de Octubre, then here. |
| 1366 | 2-8-0 | Baldwin | 1919 | 52103 | Built as 30 inch gauge Central Senado No. 12. |
| 1420 | 2-8-0 | Baldwin | 1920 | 53847 | Built as 3-foot gauge Central San Augustin No. 8. |
| 1542 | 2-8-0 | Baldwin | 1916 | 44065 | Built as C & M No. 8. Remains parked on spur after deadly boiler explosion in 1991. |

Also has 4 green diesels with V-12 motors and 420 hp. This mill has one of the most interesting and historic railroad operations in Cuba. Until 1971 it was part of a system linked by the common carrier Caibarien & Moron Railway, which hauled freight, passengers and sugar cane over the uncommon gauge of 27 1/2 inches (some say the line is actually 27 3/4 inches). Built in the 1890's, part of the original mainline is still used by Obdulio Morales trains to reach several sugar reloads, passing through quaint country villages along the way. A branch line connects this mill with its neighbor of the same gauge, Central Simon Bolivar. The traffic exchange between them is sometimes quite interesting and photogenic, often involving several steam engines at the same time. Some of these engines were built new for the mainline railway. This narow gauge operation was scheduled for conversion to standard gauge some years ago, but money ran out and left only a stretch of dual gauge on which no standard gauge trains have yet run. Regular tank car trains of molasses are hauled by steam to a feed plant behind Central Simon Bolivar.

*Right: Highball on the old mainline, as Central Obdulio Morales No. 1333 heads home with a fresh load of sugarcane, topping the same steep upgrade it used back in 1919, when Baldwin sent it new as Caibarien & Moron Railway No. 16. Part of the original C&M mainline is still used by Obdulio Morales trains, including this section from Cambao to the mill.*
IHW Photo

## Primero de Mayo (Perseverancia) Cienfuegos

| | | | | | |
|---|---|---|---|---|---|
| 1428 | 2-6-0 | BLW | 1916 | 44340 | Built as Hershey Railway No. 1 - derelict. |
| 1543 | 2-8-0 | Alco | | | |
| 1544 | 2-8-0 | Alco | 1920 | | |
| 1545 | 2-6-0 | BLW | 1915 | 42347 | Built for this mill as No. 7. |
| 1546 | 2-6-0 | BLW | 1915 | 42348 | Built for this mill as No. 9 - derelict. |
| 1848 | 2-8-0 | BLW | 1923 | 57407 | |

**Mill uses diesels, with steam mainly for switching and short runs. Also has a home-made rail truck, with couplers for switching, chain driven trolley trucks, and a steam locomotive cab.**

## Quintin Banderas (Ramona) Villa Clara

| | | | | | |
|---|---|---|---|---|---|
| 1547 | 2-6-2 | Alco | 1920 | 62096 | |
| 1548 | 4-6-0 | Alco | 1914 | 54843 | Built as Havana Central RR No.72 |

.**Two standard gauge engines alternate mill switching. Diesels work line reloads. 3-foot narrow gauge line recently abandoned. 0-4-0T No. 2 is preserved, the rest derelict or scrapped.**

## Marcelo Salado (Reforma) Villa Clara

| | | | | | |
|---|---|---|---|---|---|
| 1147 | 0-4-0ST | Davenport | 1919 | 1738 | Built for this mill as No. 5. |
| 1148 | 0-6-0ST | Alco | 1925 | 58942 | Built as 30" gauge 0-6-0T for use in Russia. Unsold, rebuilt by Cooke to standard gauge, then sold to this mill as No. 7. |
| 1342 | 4-6-0 | BLW | 1911 | 37172 | Built for this mill as No.3. |
| 1343 | 2-6-2ST | BLW | 1904 | 24614 | Received overhaul in 1995. |
| 1429 | 2-6-0 | BLW | 1916 | 44237 | Built for this mill as No. 6. |
| 1549 | 2-8-0 | Alco | 1920 | 62620 | Built for this mill as No. 8. |
| 1688 | 2-8-0 | Alco | 1925 | 66543 | Being rebuilt. |

**A classic American shortline roster, similar to Central Jose Smith Comas in upkeep of motive power, including red and white trim. Tankers switch the big, open millyard. Larger power reaches sugar reloads on branch lines by running over FCC tracks at mainline speeds. Adjacent highway allows pacing between the mill at Caibarien and the historic town of Remedios, where steam trains pass in front of the fine old station. Has operated tourist excursions with borrowed FCC heavyweight coaches. No diesels at this big, active mill. Easy to find, at the edge of Caibarien.**

*One of Cuba's largest and most modern sugar mills is Central Marcelo Salado, located just outside the port town of Caibarien, with its system of unusually well-maintained tracks that includes part of the local F.C.C. line. Among its clean motive power is yard switcher No. 1147 (at left), an 0-4-0 saddle-tanker built by Davenport in 1919, and road engine No. 1342 (on the right), a handsome Baldwin Ten-Wheeler built for this mill in 1911 as Central Reforma No. 3. It has just brought in the load of cane seen at the left and is about to retrieve its yellow caboose, in the background center.*
A&OHW Photo

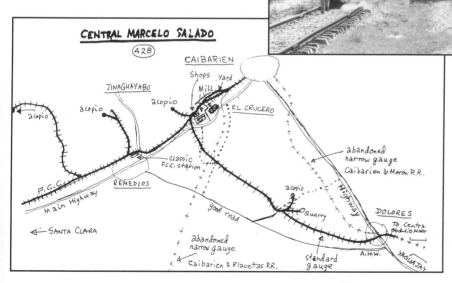

**CENTRAL MARCELO SALADO**

(428)

CAIBARIEN

JINAGUAYABO

Shops  Yard

Mill

acopio     acopio

acopio

EL CRUCERO

abandoned narrow gauge
Caibarien & Morón R.R.

classic F.C.C. station

REMEDIOS

F.C.C.

Main Highway

acopio

Quarry

Highway

DOLORES

To Central Obdulio Morón

← SANTA CLARA

good road

abandoned narrow gauge
Caibarien & Placetas R.R.

standard gauge

A.H.W.

YAGUAJAY

*Trains of Cuba*

**434**
*Standard Gauge*

## Panchito Gomez Toro (San Isidro) Villa Clara

| 1626 | 2-6-0 | BLW | 1914 |
|------|-------|-----|------|
| 1633 | 2-6-0 | BLW | 1920 |

Steam for mill switching only. 30" narrow gauge line now abandoned. One narrow gauge Baldwin Mogul still on hand, but derelict.

**435** *Narrow Gauge 3-foot*

## Hermanos Ameijeiras (San Jose) Villa Clara

| 1 | 2-6-0 | BLW | 1887 | 8956 | Built as Zozaya & Co. No. 1, also named "Adela." |
|------|-------|-----|------|-------|----------------|
| 1323 | 2-8-0 | BLW | 1920 | 53633 | Derelict. |
| 1373 | 2-8-0 | BLW | 1925 | 58755 | |
| 1431 | 2-8-0 | BLW | 1925 | 58778 | Built for this mill as No. 6. Recently rebuilt. |
| 1667 | 2-8-0 | BLW | 1920 | 54009 | |

This is the last big 3-foot gauge operation in Cuba that still has active steam, although most of the work is handled by five British made Brush diesels, nicely painted in yellow with silver and black. The steam roster includes a handsome 1887 Baldwin Mogul, with sister engines in Cuba, Colombia and the U.S. The engine was cosmetically restored recently for display, but continues to reside behind the engine house. Three fine Consolidations take turns switching the mill yard. One of several mills that used to be connected to the 3-foot gauge common carrier Placetas & Caibarien Railroad. Mainline runs south-east from mill. Steep grade about 5 miles out requires all trains to double or triple the hill on returning with loads.

*Shop foreman Armando Barnada Carvajal is justifiably proud of No. 1431, at left, which crews at Central Hermanos Ameijeiras have maintained since its arrival from Philadelphia in 1925. The Baldwin 2-8-0 takes turns with two slightly huskier sisters in switching the mill yard of this busy 3-foot gauge system near the city of Santa Clara. The shop crew is standing in front of the two-stall engine house - unusual for being fully enclosed - and their prized locomotive No. 1, a Baldwin Mogul built in 1887.*
AHW Photo

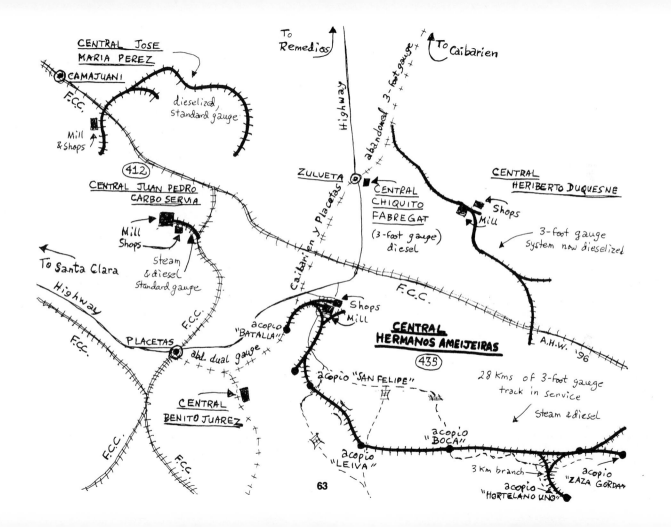

CENTRAL JOSE MARIA PEREZ

CAMAJUANI

F.C.C.

Mill & Shops

dieselized, standard gauge

To Remedios

To Caibarien

abandoned 3-foot gauge

Highway

412

CENTRAL JUAN PEDRO CARBO SERVIA

Mill Shops

steam & diesel standard gauge

To Santa Clara

Highway

F.C.C.

PLACETAS

F.C.C.

abd. dual gauge

F.C.C.

F.C.C.

CENTRAL BENITO JUAREZ

ZULUETA

CENTRAL CHIQUITO FABREGAT (3-foot gauge) diesel

Caibarien y Placetas

F.C.C.

CENTRAL HERIBERTO DUQUESNE

Shops

Mill

3-foot gauge system now dieselized

Shops Mill

CENTRAL HERMANOS AMEIJEIRAS

435

A.H.W. '96

acopio "BATALLA"

acopio "SAN FELIPE"

28 Kms of 3-foot gauge track in service

steam & diesel

acopio "BOCA"

acopio "LEIVA"

acopio "HORTELANO UNO"

3 Km branch

acopio "ZAZA GORDA"

63

*Among the best-maintained locomotives in Cuba is Central Carlos Carabello No. 1550, a handsome Baldwin Mogul built for this mill in 1920 as Central Santa Catalina No. 1. The engine is hard at work with a full load of cane, coming upgrade and ready to cross the highway from Santa Clara to Cienfuegos before entering the adjacent mill grounds. No. 1550 and sister Mogul 1556 are normally kept on standby under a covered shed, brought out mainly for charters or when a diesel breaks down.*
A&IHW Photo

**437**                                    *Standard Gauge*
## Carlos Carabello (Santa Catalina) Villa Clara

| 1550 | 2-6-0 | BLW | 1920 | 53638 | Built for this mill as No. 1. |
|------|-------|-----|------|-------|---------------|
| 1556 | 2-6-0 | BLW | 1920 | 53587 | |

**Normally dieselized, this mill occasionally surprises visitors by working its Mogul No 1, as well maintained as any locomotive in Cuba, with a white smokebox and edging, plus red trim. The mill is right beside the highway, just south of Santa Clara on the way to Cienfuegos, and is usually checked out in passing by visitors headed for more distant mills. There's a real** battle as the old Mogul struggles to haul its train of loads upgrade for the last mile or so into the mill. Sometimes sends its cane to Central Ifrain Alfonso.

**438**                                    *Standard Gauge*
## Ramon Ponciana (Santa Isabel) Sancti Spiritus

| 1552 | 4-6-0 | Alco | | | Recent overhaul. |
|------|-------|------|------|-------|---------|
| 1634 | 2-6-0 | BLW | 1920 | 54327 | |

**Mostly diesel worked, but one engine usually kept steamed for switching and stand-by.**

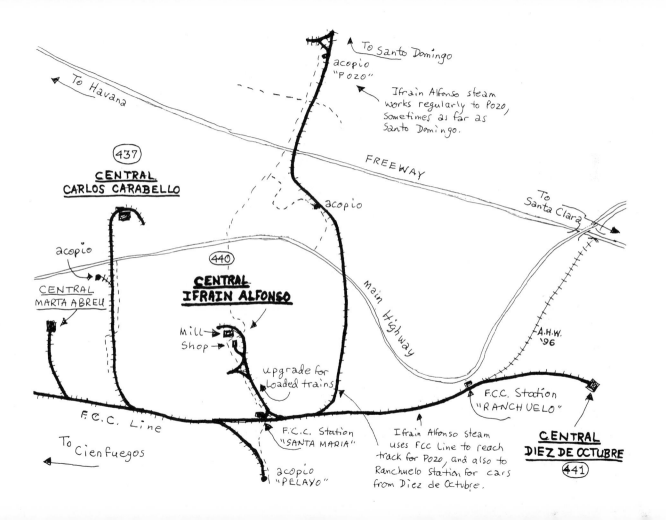

To Santo Domingo

acopio "POZO"

Ifrain Alfonso steam works regularly to Pozo, sometimes as far as Santo Domingo.

To Havana

FREEWAY

To Santa Clara

(437)
**CENTRAL CARLOS CARABELLO**

acopio

acopio

CENTRAL MARTA ABREU

(440)
**CENTRAL IFRAIN ALFONSO**

Main Highway

A.H.W. '96

Mill Shop

upgrade for loaded trains

F.C.C. Station "RANCHUELO"

F.C.C. Line

F.C.C. Station "SANTA MARIA"

Ifrain Alfonso steam uses FCC Line to reach track for Pozo, and also to Ranchuelo Station for cars from Diez de Octubre.

**CENTRAL DIEZ DE OCTUBRE**
(441)

To Cienfuegos

acopio "PELAYO"

*Cuba's Mightiest! Central Ifrain Alfonso, south of Santa Clara, defied the course of history by taking not one, but two rusting steam locomotives waiting to be scrapped,, and rebuilding them for regular service. To top off this feat, they happen to be the largest steam engines now running in Cuba, and also the country's only operating 2-8-2 Mikados. In front is No. 1850, named by crews "Dona Bella," built by Baldwin in 1935 as Banes Railroad No. 112, followed by No. 1910, named "Donna Flor," built by Alco-Brooks in 1925 as Cuba Railroad No. 351.* AHW Photo

## 440             *Standard Gauge*
### Ifrain Alfonso (Santa Maria) Villa Clara

| | | | | | |
|---|---|---|---|---|---|
| 1635 | 2-6-2 | BLW | 1925 | 58556 | Built for this mill as No. 1. |
| 1636 | 4-6-0 | Alco | 1920 | 62413 | Built for this mill. |
| 1637 | 2-8-0 | Alco | 1925 | 66432 | |
| 1850 | 2-8-2 | BLW | 1935 | 61888 | Built as Banes RR No. 112. |
| 1910 | 2-8-2 | Alco-Brooks | 1925 | 66284 | Built as Cuba RR No. 351. |

Another classic assortment of shortline locomotives, well maintained and hard working. All trains leaving the mill must receive dispatcher permission to run on FCC tracks in order to reach sugar branches to the reloads. This is especially noteworthy for the two Mikados, which used to work on mainline railroads. They are now Cuba's biggest active steam engines. Some Alfonso trackage is parallel to dirt roads, for those who want the thrill of pacing a car right alongside a regularly-slipping Mikado. A friendly mill, with much action and photo potential. A steep grade leads up from the FCC junction towards the mill.

## 441             *Standard Gauge*
### Diez de Octubre (Santa Rosa) Villa Clara

| | | | | |
|---|---|---|---|---|
| 1661 | 2-8-0 | BLW | 1925 | 58539 |
| 1818 | 2-8-0 | Alco | 1921 | 62961 |

Mostly dieselized, but steam used for switching and sometimes for hauling cane to Central Ifrain Alfonso, where steam engines also need to go for fuel oil. Trains pass Ranchuelo station on the way down the FCC line. Mill also runs an old railbus to this station for the convenience of workers.

## 446
### Carlos Balino (Ulacia) Villa Clara     *Standard Gauge*

| | | | | |
|---|---|---|---|---|
| 1432 | 4-6-0 | BLW | 1925 | 58778 |
| 1439 | 2-8-0 | Vulcan | 1913 | 2252 |
| 1555 | 4-6-0 | BLW | 1918 | 50995 |
| 1643 | 4-6-0 | BLW | 1917 | 45925 |

Partly dieselized; runs south past the FCC station in the nearby town of Santo Domingo. Has a nice, short, wooden caboose.

## 447             *Standard Gauge*
### Unidad Proleteria (Unidad) Villa Clara

| | | | | | |
|---|---|---|---|---|---|
| 1346 | 0-6-0ST | Vulcan | 1917 | 2604 | Derelict |
| 1595 | 2-6-0 | Vulcan | 1917 | 2711 | Derelict |
| 1823 | 2-8-0 | Alco | 1920 | 62042 | Built as United Railways of Havana No. 306. |

*Trains of Cuba*

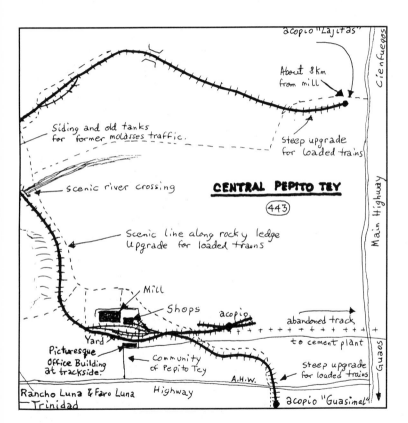

Map labels:
- acopio "Lajitas"
- Cienfuegos
- About 8 km from mill
- Siding and old tanks for former molasses traffic.
- Steep upgrade for loaded trains
- Scenic river crossing
- **CENTRAL PEPITO TEY**
- (443)
- Main Highway
- Scenic line along rocky ledge Upgrade for loaded trains
- Mill
- Shops
- acopio
- abandoned track
- to cement plant
- Yard
- Picturesque Office Building at trackside.
- Community of Pepito Tey
- Guaos
- steep upgrade for loaded trains
- A.H.W.
- Rancho Luna & Faro Luna - Trinidad
- Highway
- acopio "Guasimal"

**443** — *Narrow Gauge 30"*

**Pepito Tey (Soledad) Cienfuegos**

| | | | | | |
|---|---|---|---|---|---|
| 1162 | 2-8-0 | BLW | 1916 | 44286 | Built as Cuban Central RR No. 36. Derelict. |
| 1164 | 2-6-0 | BLW | 1919 | 52163 | Built new for this mill as No. 7. |
| 1165 | 2-6-0 | BLW | 1924 | 57946 | Built new for this mill as No. 8. |
| 1220 | 2-8-0 | BLW | 1910 | 35782 | Built for mill at Mal Tiempo as No. 6. |
| 1236 | 2-8-0 | BLW | 1910 | 35459 | |
| 1330 | 2-8-0 | BLW | 1916 | 43851 | Derelict |
| 1337 | 2-8-0 | BLW | 1919 | 52236 | |
| 1357 | 2-8-0 | BLW | 1909 | 33553 | Built new for this mill and named "Aramao." |
| 1358 | 2-8-0 | BLW | 1915 | 42136 | Built new for this mill as No. 6. |

A photogenic and busy operation with several of its original engines on the all-steam roster. Located just a short drive from tourist resorts around the city of Cienfuegos. One of the last narrow gauge lines to use Moguls, although one of the pair was recently retired, its yard switching taken over by No. 1220, a new arrival from nearby Central Mal Tiempo. At one time it was proposed to electrify this line, then more recently to convert it for standard gauge, but it remains all steam and 2 1/2 foot gauge.

*Opposite: "Living Museum" would be a good description for the locomotive shops of Central Pepito Tey, where one of the narrow gauge Baldwin Consolidations is in for quick running repairs while another receives a total overhaul in the background. Tools and methods are seemingly from another era, but used for daily work rather than for museum preservation.*
A&OHW Photo

## Simon Bolivar (Vitoria) Sancti Spiritus

| Simon | Bolivar | (Vitoria) | Sancti | Spiritus | |
|---|---|---|---|---|---|
| 1138 | 2-6-0 | Baldwin | 1908 | 33067 | Built as Caibarien & Moron Ry No. 6. |
| 1166 | 2-6-0 | Baldwin | 1891 | 12272 | Built as C & M 0-6-4T No. 1A. Derelict. |
| 1167 | 2-4-0 | Baldwin | 1905 | 25264 | Built as FC Yaguajay No. 1 (a nearby town). Another rare treasure, also derelict. |
| 1244 | 2-8-0 | Baldwin | 1892 | 13021 | C & M No. 2. Dismantled for parts. |
| 1361 | 2-8-0 | BLW | 1920 | 53064 | Built for this railroad as No 6. |
| 1362 | 2-8-0 | Vulcan | 1919 | 2984 | Built as 30 inch gauge Central Azu Sagua No. 11. Overhauled in 1996 and now the only narrow gauge Vulcan working in Cuba. |
| 1363 | 2-8-0 | Baldwin | 1917 | 46768 | Built as C & M No. 9, named "Aime," then "Antonio Guiteras." |
| 1367 | 2-8-0 | Baldwin | 1924 | | Built as 30 inch gauge for Central Senado. |

Mill also has 3 orange diesels with V-12 motors, plus two classic rail-trucks for track work. This mill has a very photogenic shop and yard area, where one of Cuba's few remaining narrow gauge Moguls does the regular switching. Much more exciting - and difficult to reach - is the Loma section of its main-line, which has steep grades and sharp curves

that wind their way through rugged wilderness. The two rail-trucks are of special note, photogenic in the style of those in Colorado. The trains of this mill meet trains from Obdulio Morales at an interesting junction located in the village of Centeno and controlled by a semaphore system.

*Memories of the Colorado Rockies are evoked by this Caribbean version of the famed Galloping Goose. Shop crews at Central Simon Bolivar built these two rail-trucks using parts from earlier rigs built in the U.S. They are now powered by Russian tractor motors, using chain drive and a braking system operated by turning the steering wheel.*
IHW Photo

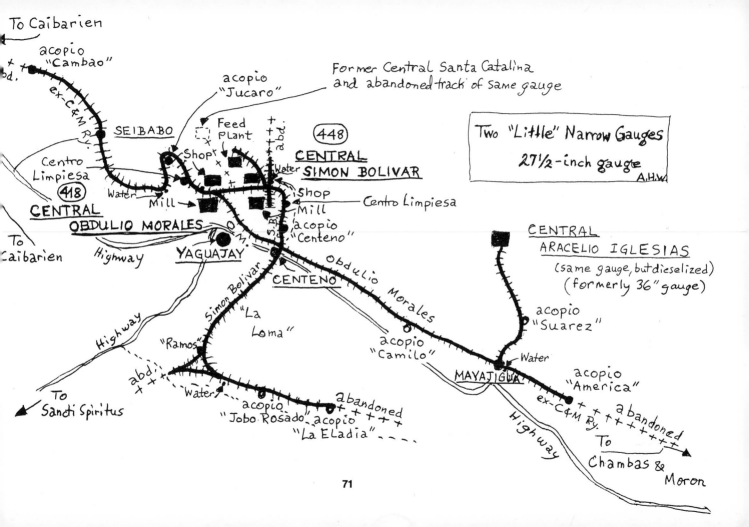

To Caibarien

acopio "Cambao"

abd.

ex-C&M Ry.

SEIBABO

acopio "Jucaro"

Feed Plant

Shop

abd.

Former Central Santa Catalina and abandoned track of same gauge

448

CENTRAL SIMON BOLIVAR

Two "Little" Narrow Gauges 27½-inch gauge

A.H.W.

Centro Limpiesa

418

CENTRAL OBDULIO MORALES

Water

Mill

Water

Shop

Mill

acopio "Centeno"

Centro Limpiesa

CENTRAL ARACELIO IGLESIAS

(same gauge, but dieselized)

(formerly 36" gauge)

To Caibarien

Highway

YAGUAJAY

CENTENO

Simon Bolivar

"La Loma"

Obdulio Morales

acopio "Camilo"

acopio "Suarez"

Highway

"Ramos"

abd.

Water

acopio "Jobo Rosado"

acopio "La Eladia"

abandoned

MAYAJIGUA

Water

acopio "America"

ex-C&M Ry.

abandoned

To Sancti Spiritus

Highway

To Chambas & Moron

71

**449**                                          *Standard Gauge*

**George Washington (Washington) Villa Clara**

| | | | | | |
|---|---|---|---|---|---|
| 1 | 0-4-0T | | | | A rare, old steam dummy. Derelict. |
| 2 | 2-6-0 | BLW | | | Derelict. |
| 1168 | 0-4-0T | O&K | 1924 | 1067 | Derelict. |
| 1632 | 4-6-0 | Alco | 1914 | 54836 | Derelict. Built as Havana Central RR No. 65. |
| 1639 | 2-8-0 | Alco | 1919 | 58778 | |
| 1644 | 2-8-0 | Alco | 1913 | 54366 | Built as Cuban Central RR No. 111. |

**503**                                          *Standard Gauge*

**Orlando Gonzales Ramirez (Algodones) Ciego de Avila**

| | | | | | |
|---|---|---|---|---|---|
| 1562 | 2-6-0 | BLW | 1920 | 53805 | Derelict. |
| 1563 | 2-6-0 | BLW | 1920 | 53877 | |
| 1732 | 4-6-0 | Alco | 1916 | 55991 | Built as Cuba RR No. 243. |
| 1736 | 4-6-0 | Alco | 1920 | 62655 | Built as Cuban Central RR No. 121. |
| 1836 | 2-8-0 | Vulcan | 1922 | 3148 | |
| 1837 | 2-8-0 | Alco | 1920 | 62543 | Built for this mill as No. 2. |

**504**                                          *Standard Gauge*

**Ecuador (Baragua) Ciego de Avila**

| | | | | | |
|---|---|---|---|---|---|
| 1564 | 2-6-0 | Vulcan | 1916 | 2449 | Built for this mill as No. 1. |
| 1649 | 2-6-0 | BLW | 1919 | 52423 | |
| 1817 | 2-8-0 | Alco | 1919 | 58784 | |
| 1821 | 2-8-0 | BLW | 1920 | 52944 | |
| 1904 | 2-8-0 | Vulcan | 1920 | 3102 | Reboilered 1991 |

**Lots of steam action, though railway is difficult to follow by road.**

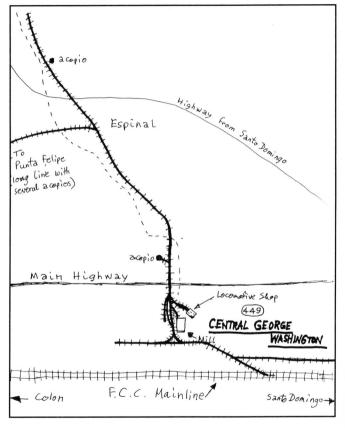

*Twilight Zone in the world of railroading. A local farmer races across the tracks while a star-decorated tractor waits for the passing of the little tank engine that is switching the yard at Central Jose Smith Comas. The well maintained 0-4-0T was built by Porter in 1909 and carries the Minaz number of 1122. Amazingly, this scene was photographed just fifteen minutes - yet seemingly a whole world - away from the crowded resort hotels and beaches of Varadero.*
IHW Photo

*Trains of Cuba*

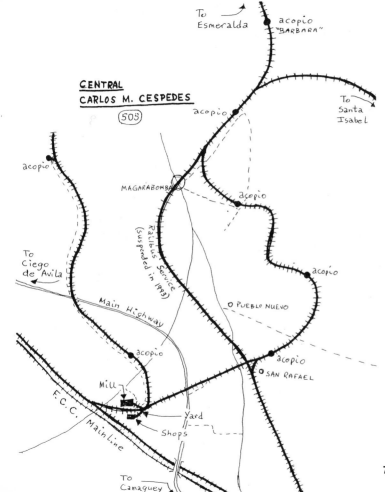

CENTRAL
CARLOS M. CESPEDES
(505)

To Esmeralda
acopio "BARBARA"
acopio
To Santa Isabel
acopio
acopio
MAGARABOMBA
acopio
Railbus Service (suspended in 1993)
To Ciego de Avila
Main Highway
O PUEBLO NUEVO
acopio
acopio
O SAN RAFAEL
Mill
F.C.C. Mainline
Yard
Shops
To Camaguey

**505**                                                   *Standard Gauge*

## Carlos Manuel de Cespedes (Cespedes) Camaguey

| | | | | | |
|---|---|---|---|---|---|
| 1173 | 0-4-0ST | BLW | 1915 | 42761 | Built for this mill as No. 1. |
| 1174 | 0-4-0ST | Davenport | 1919 | 1737 | Derelict. |
| 1444 | 2-6-0 | Porter | 1919 | 6227 | Built for this mill as No. 6. Derelict. |
| 1445 | 2-6-2 | BLW | 1920 | 53594 | |
| 1567 | 4-6-0 | Pittsburgh | 1896 | 1592 | Built as Pittsburgh & Lake Erie No. 82. Derelict. |
| 1744 | 2-6-0 | Vulcan | 1921 | 3154 | Built as Cuba Northern RR 0-6-0 No. P3. |
| 1746 | 2-8-0 | BLW | 1920 | 54076 | |
| 1838 | 2-8-0 | BLW | 1919 | 52481 | Built as Cuba Northern RR No. 48. |
| 1843 | 2-8-0 | BLW | 1924 | 57866 | Derelict. |
| 1906 | 2-8-0 | BLW | 1920 | 53657 | Built for this mill as No. 5. |
| 1907 | 2-8-0 | BLW | 1924 | 57865 | Built for this mill as No. 6. |

This mid island mill used to be one of the biggest steam operators, but diesels have arrived in recent years and steam is now limited mostly to yard switching and short runs to the nearest reloads. Great variety in locomotive builders and wheel arrangements. Note the rare Pittsburgh Ten-Wheeler that ran on the Pittsburgh & Lake Erie RR as No. 82 in the 1890s.

*Opposite: Track crew takes a break while Consolidation No. 1838 switches the mill yard lead at Central Carlos M. Cespedes. This handsome 2-8-0 was built by Baldwin in 1919 for mainline service as Cuba Northern Railroad No. 48.*
A&BHW Photo

74

**75**

*Trains of Cuba*

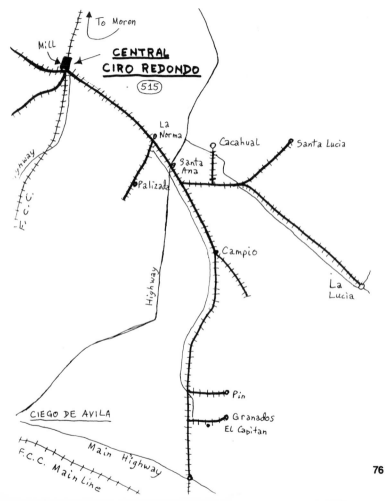

To Moron

Mill

**CENTRAL**
**CIRO REDONDO**
(515)

La Norma

Cacahual

Santa Lucia

Santa Ana

Palizada

Highway
F.C.C.

Campio

La Lucia

Highway

CIEGO DE AVILA

Pin

Granados
El Capitan

Main Highway

F.C.C. Main Line

---

**506**                                                              *Standard Gauge*

**Bolivia (Cunagua)  Ciego de Avila**

| | | | | | |
|---|---|---|---|---|---|
| 1169 | 0-4-0F | BLW | 1917 | 46254 | Built for this mill as No. 3. |
| 1170 | 0-4-0F | BLW | 1916 | 42842 | |
| 1171 | 0-4-0F | BLW | 1920 | 53100 | Built for this mill as No. 9. |
| 1172 | 0-4-0F | O&K | 1912 | 5083 | |

**A quartet of fireless engines work as mill-yard switchers.**

**511**                                                              *Standard Gauge*

**Brasil (Jaronu)  Camaguey**

| | | | | | |
|---|---|---|---|---|---|
| 1250 | 0-6-0F | Henschel | 1924 | 20380 | Built for this mill. |
| 1251 | 0-4-0F | BLW | 1927 | 60099 | Built for this mill as No. 57. |
| 1368 | 0-4-0F | BLW | 1920 | 53876 | Built for this mill as No. 55. |
| 1369 | 0-4-0F | BLW | 1920 | 53832 | Built for this mill as No. 51. |
| 1370 | 0-6-0F | Henschel | 1923 | 20120 | |

**Similar to Central Bolivia, but five engines instead of four.**

**515**                                                              *Standard Gauge*

**Ciro Redondo (Moron)  Ciego de Avila**

| | | | | | |
|---|---|---|---|---|---|
| 1826 | 2-8-0 | Alco | 1921 | 62960 | |
| 1827 | 2-8-0 | BLW | 1920 | 52945 | |
| 1828 | 2-8-0 | BLW | 1920 | 52970 | |
| 1830 | 2-8-0 | BLW | 1920 | 52973 | |
| 1831 | 2-8-0 | BLW | 1920 | 53920 | Derelict. |
| 1832 | 2-8-0 | BLW | 1920 | 53952 | |
| 1833 | 2-8-0 | BLW | 1922 | 57404 | Derelict. |
| 1834 | 2-8-0 | BLW | 1919 | 52539 | |

**Also operates an interesting homemade railtruck.**

## 520

**Noel Fernandez (Senado) Camaguey** — *Standard Gauge*

| 1568 | 2-6-0 | Vulcan | 1916 | 2577 | Built for this mill as No. 11. |
|------|-------|--------|------|------|--------------------------------|
| 1658 | 2-8-0 | Vulcan | 1920 | 3104 | |
| 1664 | 2-8-0 | BLW | 1920 | 53521 | Built for this mill as No. 14. |
| 1844 | 2-8-0 | BLW | 1926 | 59220 | |

Steam mainly for mill switching. Displayed near mill is its former No 2, an 1882 Porter 0-4-2T of 30 inch gauge. Note that Nos. 1658 and 1664 are now fireless conversions, the only successful ones (out of several attempts) running in Cuba.

## 522

**Venezuela (Stewart) Ciego de Avila** — *Standard Gauge*

| 1657 | 4-6-0 | Alco | 1916 | 56018 | Built as Cuba RR No. 239. Said to have the tallest drivers of any engine in Cuba. |
|------|-------|------|------|-------|----------------------------------------------------------------------------------|
| 1738 | 4-6-0 | BLW | 1918 | 50735 | Built as Cuba Northern RR No. 29. |
| 1739 | 2-8-0 | BLW | 1920 | 52943 | |
| 1740 | 2-8-0 | BLW | 1920 | 52971 | |
| 1741 | 2-8-0 | BLW | 1920 | 52972 | |
| 1742 | 2-8-0 | BLW | 1920 | 53853 | Built for this mill as No. 16. |
| 1743 | 2-8-0 | BLW | 1920 | 53854 | Built for this mill as No. 17. |
| 1825 | 2-8-0 | Alco | 1925 | 65190 | |
| 1902 | 2-8-0 | Vulcan | 1920 | 3004 | Built as Cuba Northern RR No. 45. |

Lines are south-east, south, and west of mill. Lots of grades and heavy action. Also has a couple of interesting trackwork trolleys.

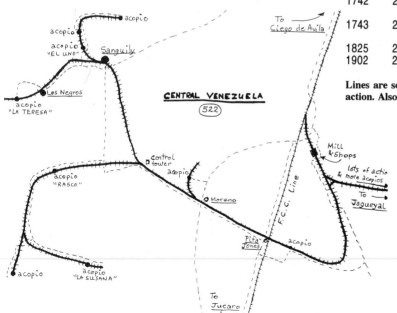

CENTRAL VENEZUELA
(522)

*Cuban sugar railroading as seen from the tender of Central Bartolome Maso 2-8-0 No. 1589 as it pushes a string of cars towards the sugar mill. This and several nearby operations in the province of Granma are not often visited or photographed because of their relatively remote locations. In addition, mills on the eastern end of the island began dieselizing earlier, so that steam action at most of them is now only sporadic, or else gone.*
Wildy Photo

## 615
## Bartolome Maso (Estrada Palma)  Granma

*Standard Gauge*

| | | | | | |
|---|---|---|---|---|---|
| 1590 | 2-8-0 | Alco | 1926 | 65196 | Built for this mill as No. 4. |
| 1757 | 2-8-0 | BLW | 1920 | 54226 | |

Sporadic operation at this remote mill in recent years
.

## 620
## Arquimedes Colina (Mabay)  Granma

*Standard Gauge*

| | | | | |
|---|---|---|---|---|
| 1384 | 2-6-0 | | 1920 | |
| 1582 | 2-8-0 | BLW | 1920 | 53856 |
| 1588 | 2-8-0 | Alco | 1923 | 65276 |
| 1589 | 2-8-0 | Alco | 1926 | 65195 |
| 1675 | 2-6-0 | BLW | 1923 | 57384 |

Limited steam action, with diesels on hand. Also has two dieselized steam conversions, an 0-4-0T and a 2-6-0.

## 621
## Antonio Maceo (Maceo)  Holguin

*Standard Gauge*

| | | | | | |
|---|---|---|---|---|---|
| 1586 | 2-8-0 | Alco | | | Assumed to have been built for this mill. |
| 1681 | 2-8-0 | BLW | 1920 | 53884 | |
| 1756 | 2-8-0 | BLW | 1925 | 58496 | |

Dieselized, with steam only in reserve.

## 627
## Jose N. Figueredo (Rio Cuato)  Granma

*Standard Gauge*

| | | | | | |
|---|---|---|---|---|---|
| 1455 | 2-6-0 | Vulcan | 1942 | 4395 | Built as Nicaro Nickel Co. 0-6-0T No. 2. |
| 1676 | 4-6-0 | BLW | 1920 | 53349 | |
| 1677 | 4-6-0 | BLW | 1918 | 50785 | Built as Cuba Northern RR No. 31. |

Limited steam, with diesels. Mogul 1455 is the newest steam locomotive operating in Cuba.

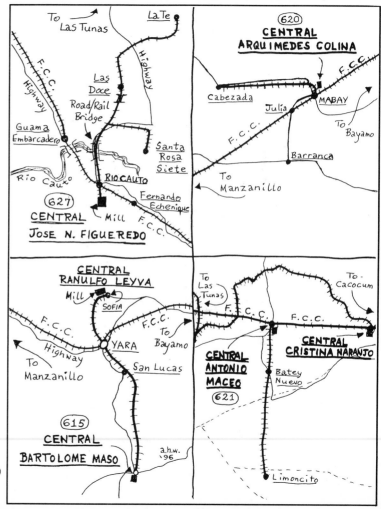

**Rafael Freyre (Santa Lucia) Holguin**                                *Narrow Gauge 30"*

| | | | | | |
|---|---|---|---|---|---|
| 1 | 0-6-0 | BLW | 1882 | 6456 | Built for this area as Ingenio Santa Lucia No. 1. |
| 5 | 2-6-0 | BLW | 1924 | 57797 | Transferred from Central Paraguay, but found unsuitable. Derelict. |
| 1385 | 2-8-0 | BLW | 1919 | 52380 | Built for this mill as Santa Lucia No. 10. Named "Arroyo Blanco." |
| 1386 | 2-8-0 | BLW | 1919 | 52630 | Built for this mill as Santa Lucia No.4. Named "Guabaja-ney." |
| 1387 | 2-8-0 | BLW | 1905 | 26416 | Built for this mill as Santa Lucia No. 5. Named "Vita." |
| 1388 | 2-8-0 | BLW | 1907 | 31375 | Built for this mill as Santa Lucia No. 6. Named "Junocun." |
| 1389 | 2-8-0 | BLW | 1912 | 37716 | Built for this mill as Santa Lucia No 7. Named "Giron." |
| 1390 | 2-8-0 | BLW | 1912 | 38101 | Built for this mill as Santa Lucia No. 8. Named "Yagua-jay." |
| 1391 | 2-8-0 | BLW | 1914 | 41468 | Built for this mill as Santa Lucia No. 9. Named "Camay-en." |

"Cuba's Rio Grande Southern" operates in two scenic directions from the mill and old company town of Santa Lucia, in the remote northeast corner of Cuba - though only minutes from several fine Atlantic coast hotels around Guardelavaca. Trains are worked by steam on a "mountain division" that includes a couple of dramatic branchlines. Diesels do yard switching and bring in light cane loads from the easier places, but usually two or three of the line's original steam engines are out on the road every day. Very photogenic railroad with friendly crews and people. A noteable roster of original steam, all in working order. 1883 Baldwin 0-6-0 No. 2 from this mill is currently displayed in nearby Banes.

*Among Cuba's most precious operable locomotives is this 30-inch gauge Baldwin 0-6-0 built in 1882 and here being fired up at Central Rafael Freyre. The well kept midget even makes the facing little 2-8-0 look big.*
A&OHW Photo

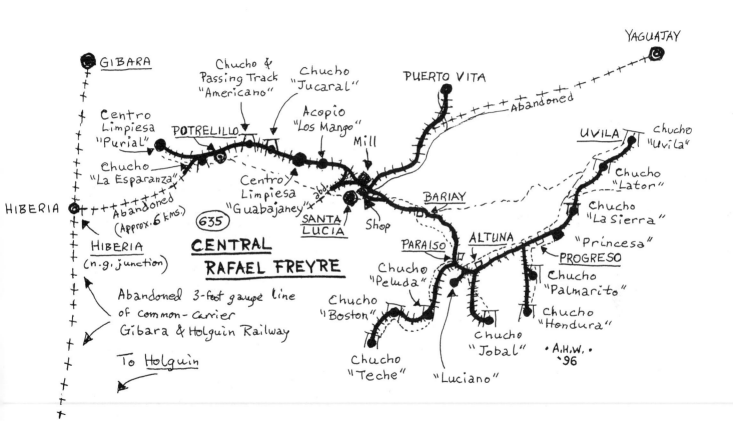

GIBARA

YAGUAJAY

PUERTO VITA

Chucho &
Passing Track
"Americano"

Chucho
"Jucaral"

UVILA          Chucho
               "Uvila"

Centro
Limpiesa
"Purial"

POTRELILLO

Acopio
"Los Mango"

Mill

Chucho
"Lator"

Chucho
"La Esparanza"

Centro
Limpiesa
"Guabajaney"

Abandoned

Chucho
"La Sierra"

HIBERIA

Abandoned
(Approx. 6 kms.)

abd.

BARIAY

"Princesa"

635

SANTA
LUCIA

Shop

PROGRESO

Chucho
"Palmarito"

HIBERIA
(n.g. junction)

CENTRAL
RAFAEL FREYRE

PARAISO        ALTUNA

Chucho
"Peluda"

Chucho
"Honduro"

Abandoned 3-foot gauge line
of common-carrier
Gibara & Holguin Railway

Chucho
"Boston"

Chucho
"Jobal"

· A.H.W. ·
'96

To Holguin

Chucho
"Teche"

"Luciano"

*Above: Cuba received several used locomotives from sugar mills in Hawaii that shut down their railroad operations in the 1940's and 50's, including the yellow and green GE centercab diesel unit seen here from the tender of Rafael Freyre No. 1 (on opposite page). No. 2413 and a twin were built for 3-foot gauge by General Electric in 1939, then converted in Cuba to 30". The engine is seen switching the caboose track in the Rafael Freyre millyard.*
*Opposite: What other railroad in the world still maintains its original No. 1 locomotive after well over 100 years? The fireman here was doing some light oiling during a photo pause, while the engine and its little passenger car were headed for the coastal village of Puerto Vita, taking the author and his son down a branchline for the railroad's first charter trip.*
Both A&OHW Photos

## 637 — Standard Gauge
### Ranulfo Leyva (Sofia) Granma

| | | | | | |
|---|---|---|---|---|---|
| 1464 | 2-6-0 | Alco | 1923 | 62625 | Built for this mill as No.1. |
| 1575 | 2-8-0 | BLW | 1920 | 54248 | |

Limited steam activity using mostly diesels.

## 640 — Narrow gauge 3 foot
### Frank Pais (Tanamo) Holguin

| | | | | | |
|---|---|---|---|---|---|
| 1254 | 2-8-0 | BLW | | | |
| 1256 | 2-8-0 | BLW | 57207 | 1923 | Built for this mill as No. 10. |
| 1458 | 4-6-0 | BLW | 53858 | 1920 | Built for this mill as No. 4. |
| 1459 | 4-6-0 | BLW | 53859 | 1920 | Built for this mill as No. 5. |

A remote and seldom visited line, mostly using various vintage GE diesels, but notable for its pair of sisters to the widely famous Tweetsie ten-wheelers in the American south.

## 641 — Standard Gauge
### Rafael Reyes (Union) Santiago de Cuba

| | | | | | |
|---|---|---|---|---|---|
| | 0-6-0 | BLW | | | Preserved |
| 1454 | 2-6-0 | BLW | 57213 | 1923 | Built as an 0-6-0. |
| 1581 | 2-6-0 | BLW | 54969 | 1920 | Built for this mill as No. 3. |
| 1669 | 2-8-0 | Alco | 66466 | 1925 | |
| 1670 | 2-8-0 | Alco | 62507 | 1920 | Derelict. |
| 1673 | 2-8-0 | BLW | 53878 | 1920 | Derelict. |

Primarily dieselized.

*Trains of Cuba*

*Right: Engineer Dima takes a turn with the firing valve to get more power out of old No. 1386, working upgrade near La Sierra on the mountainous Rafael Freyre line.*
 AHW Photo

*Left: Brill-type railbus No. 50 still provides passenger service along some of the Rafael Freyre line. Here, its driver stands with a passenger and friend, waiting for the dispatcher's phoned permission to return from the branch at Jobal to the mill in Santa Lucia.*
 AHW Photo

*Opposite: William Jackson photographed scenes that looked like this in the Colorado Rockies during the late 1800's, but who would have thought they'd still take place 100 years later. Two narrow gauge Baldwin 2-8-0's are seen at La Caridad de Bariay on Central Rafael Freyre's scenic line.*
A&OHW Photo

*Trains of Cuba*

*Opposite: Newest steam locomotive operating in Cuba is this 1942 Vulcan-built Mogul, Central Jose N. Figueredo No. 1455, which worked originally in mining service as Nicaro Nickel Co. No. 2.*
*Above: Not far from the sea in Granma province, Central Jose N. Figueredo Baldwin-built No. 1676 is one of two similar Ten-Wheelers.* Both, Wildy Photos

*Cuba is a dream come true for young photographers who missed out on North America's steam era. Boiler repairs and running gear close-ups are among the numerous daily scenes available. These were on the line of Central Jose N. Figueredo.*
Both, Wildy Photos

*Left: While photographing trains with steam in action it's easy to forget that each old locomotive has its own characteristics and details, as in this close-up.*

*Opposite: Darkness comes fast in Cuba after an often-spectacular sunset, requiring skill, timing and luck for making good train photographs. This one shows Central Arquimedes Colina Consolidation No. 1588 coming in with a fresh load of sugarcane at twilight.*

Both, Wildy Photos

*Opposite top: Among Cuba's best maintained engines are Central Marcelo Salado No. 1342 (a Baldwin 4-6-0 from 1911) and No. 1429 (a Baldwin 2-6-0 from 1916). Both locomotives had fresh black paint, plus lots of red and white trim.*

*Opposite bottom, Although nearly two-thirds of Cuba's 156 sugar mills have no active steam, their dieselized operations often include other interesting equipment. An example is Central Dos Rios, located in a remote eastern part of the island, which provides passenger service on its network of countryside sugar lines with this fleet of standard gauge homemade railbuses, each one built and painted differently from the other.*

Both A&OHW Photos

*Above: While most sugar railroads use cabooses, few are made of wood like this little classic at Central Carlos Balino. Alco influence is obvious on diesel No. 37162, part of a fleet sent by the USSR in 1978. Plans to replace all steam have been postponed since then. Behind the caboose stands a cane-loading "chucho." (Right) Two of the stocky standard gauge Consolidations that work for Central Victoria de Yaguajay, with steel caboose No. 1440 in between.*

Both A&IHW Photos

*Trains of Cuba*

*Left: Looking from the four-stall enginehouse of Central Simon Bolivar at four of the line's 27 1/2 inch gauge locomotives.*
A&OHW Photo

*Below: One of Cuba's most unaltered old locomotives is Central Pepito Tey No. 1358, a 30-inch gauge Consolidation built by Baldwin in 1915 and still carrying its original oil-burning head-light, along with other antique parts. Due to a few greedy tourists all Pepito Tey engines are now missing their builder's plates.*
AHW Photo

*(Opposite) Hold your breath and focus on the action! Cuba is the leading place in the world for old-time American-style steam rail-roading. As an example, here's Central Espartaco's No. 1326, a 30-inch gauge Consolidation built by Baldwin in 1895 and still ca-pable of thundering down the slim tracks with a full load of fresh sugar cane. The crewman was leaning out to grab a pack of cigar-ettes from the photographers.*
IHW Photo

*Trains of Cuba*

# ★ STEAM ROSTER & MAP INDEX ★

| Name of Central | Mill No. | Locomotives | Pages |
|---|---|---|---|
| Alfonso, Ifrain | 440 | 5 S.G. | 65, 66 |
| Alvarez, Humberto | 308 | 4 N.G. | 43 |
| Ameijeiras, Hermano | 435 | 5 N.G. | 62, 63 |
| Australia | 303 | 7 S.G. | 40, 47 |
| Avila, Juan | 320 | 6 S.G. | 50 |
| Balino, Carlos | 446 | 4 S.G. | 67, 92 |
| Banderas, Quinten | 427 | 2 S.G. | 60 |
| Bergnes, Luis Arcos | 405 | 4 S.G. | 54, 55 |
| Bolivar, Simon | 448 | 8 N.G. | 31, 70, 71, 95 |
| Bolivia | 506 | 4 S.G. | 76 |
| Brasil | 511 | 5. S.G. | 76 |
| Brau, Pablo de la Torriente | 107 | 7 S.G. | 34, 35 |
| Cairo, Julio Reyes | 321 | 6 S.G. | 50, 51 |
| Carabello, Carlos | 437 | 2 S.G. | 64, 65 |
| Caracas, Ciudad | 404 | 5 S.G. | 54 |
| Cespedes, Carlos Manuel de | 505 | 11 S.G. | 74, 75 |
| Coloma, Boris Luis Santa | 212 | 6 S.G. | 38, 39 |
| Colina, Arquimedes | 620 | 5 S.G. | 79, 90, 91 |
| Comas, Jose Smith | 315 | 7 S.G. | 48, 49, 73 |
| Ecuador | 504 | 5 S.G. | 72 |
| Espartaco | 413 | 6 N.G. | 56, 57, 94 |
| Fernandez, Noel | 520 | 4 S.G. | 77 |
| Figueredo, Jose N. | 627 | 3 S.G. | 79, 86 to 89 |
| Fraga, Rene | 319 | 7 S.G. | 47, 48 |
| Freyre, Rafael | 635 | 9 N.G. | 6, 9, 80 to 85 |
| Garcia, Reynold | 302 | 3 S.G. | 47 |
| Grajales, Mariana | 408 | 1 S.G. | 54 |
| Granma | 304 | 5 S.G. | 41 |
| Lavardero, Eduardo Garcia | 103 | 5 S.G. | 34 |
| Leyva, Ranulfo | 637 | 2 S.G. | 79, 82 |
| Libre, Puerto Rico | 305 | 6 S.G. | 43 |
| Libre, Cuba | 306 | 6 S.G. | 42, 43 |
| Maceo, Antonio | 621 | 3 S.G. | 79 |
| Mal Tiempo | 403 | 7 N.G. | 52, 53 |
| Manalich, Gregorio Arlee | 207 | 9 NG. 4 S.G. | 37 |
| Maso, Bartolome | 615 | 2 S.G. | 78, 79 |
| Marti, Jose | 108 | 4 S.G. | 35 |
| Mayo, Primero de | 424 | 6 S.G. | 60 |
| Morales, Obdulio | 418 | 10 N.G. | 30, 58, 59, 71 |
| Octubre, Diez de | 441 | 2 S.G. | 65, 67 |
| Pais, Frank | 640 | 4 N.G. | 82 |
| Perez, Manuel Isla | 206 | 6 S.G. | 36 |
| Ponciana, Ramon | 438 | 2 S.G. | 64 |
| Proletaria, Unidad | 447 | 3 S.G. | 67 |
| Pueblos, Amistad Con Los | 201 | 7 S.G. | 36 |
| Rabi, Jesus | 314 | 5 S.G. | 46, 47 |
| Ramirez, Orlando Gonzalez | 503 | 5 S.G. | 72 |
| Redondo, Ciro | 515 | 8 S.G. | 76 |
| Reyes, Rafael | 641 | 6 S.G. | 82 |
| Rodriguez, Fructuoso | 312 | 4 S.G. | 44, 45 |
| Salado, Marcelo | 428 | 7 S.G. | 60, 61, 93 |
| Sanchez, Antonio | 409 | 5 S.G. | 54 |
| Sanchez, Osvaldo | 210 | 5 N.G. 2 S.G. | 38 |
| Sandino, A.C. | 105 | 9 N.G. | 34 |
| Santa Coloma, Boris Luis | 212 | 6 S.G. | 38, 39 |
| Santamaria | 407 | 1 S.G. | 54 |
| Servia, Juan Pedro Carbo | 412 | 3 S.G. | 54, 63 |
| Tey, Pepito | 443 | 9 N.G. | 30, 68, 69, 95 |
| Toro, Panchito Gomez | 434 | 2 S.G. | 62 |
| Venezuela | 522 | 12 S.G. | 77 |
| Villena, Ruben Martinez | 211 | 10 S.G. | 33, 38, 39 |
| Washington, George | 449 | 6 S.G. | 72 |
| Yaguajay, Victoria de | 318 | 5 S.G. | 41, 48, 92 |